HOUGHTON
The Birthplace of Professional Hockey

William J. Sproule

Houghton: The Birthplace of Professional Hockey

Copyright © 2019 by William J. Sproule

No part of this publication may be reproduced, or stored in a retrieval system, or transmitted in any form or by any means, mechanical, recording or otherwise, without the express written permission of the copyright holder.

Front cover image: 1903–04 Portage Lake hockey team (Michigan Technological University Archives and Copper Country Historical Collections)

Back cover: Hockey sweaters from the five IHL teams (from SIHR Sweater Museum used with permission from Danny Laflamme)

Design: Smythtype Design

ISBN-13: 978-1-7330823-0-3

Printed in U.S.A

CONTENTS

Preface 5

CHAPTER 1 – Early Hockey History 7

CHAPTER 2 – Houghton and the Copper Country 25

CHAPTER 3 – Gibson Comes to Houghton 39

CHAPTER 4 – Professional Hockey Begins in Houghton 53

CHAPTER 5 – The Original International Hockey League 65

CHAPTER 6 – Three Seasons of Professional Hockey 77

CHAPTER 7 – International Hockey League Players 91

CHAPTER 8 – After the International Hockey League 113

References 133

Preface

SEVERAL YEARS AGO I VOLUNTEERED TO TEACH A hockey history course at Michigan Tech University and as I gathered materials for the course I discovered newspaper clippings that indicated that professional hockey started in Houghton, Michigan. I also found an advertisement for a two-game series between the Montreal Wanderers, the Champions of Canada, and Portage Lake, the United States Champions, for the World's Championship to be played March 21 and 22 (1904) at the Amphidrome. For someone born and raised in Canada, I was intrigued and wanted to discover more so I spend many days reading books, articles, and old newspapers to uncover the story. I also found a group of hockey historians, the Society for International Hockey Research (SIHR), whose members have been so helpful and willing to share their enthusiasm. I have written several articles, made numerous presentations in the community, and several have encouraged me to document the story in a book. With the quote in mind that "claims of first things are never without dispute" I wanted to be confident that Houghton is the birthplace of professional hockey.

This is the story of how a Canadian-born dentist and Houghton entrepreneur changed hockey by openly paying players to come to Michigan's Copper Country to play hockey. The book explores the early hockey history in Canada and the roles that the Stanley Cup, the Ontario Hockey Association, and others played in insuring that hockey would be a game for amateurs and no one should be paid to play hockey. The book describes how the popular sports of roller polo and ice polo developed into ice hockey in the United States as Canadian teams and players introduced the game in New England, Minnesota, Pittsburgh, and Michigan's Upper Peninsula. The first stories of ice hockey in the Copper Country date back to 1897, when Canadian-born Ernest Yates organized a team of Canadians from the Hancock Chemical Company in Dollar Bay to play several exhibition games to generate interest and have teams form in the different towns in the county. Hockey did catch on and the Copper Country soon became the center for exciting ice hockey in the Midwest. New arenas opened and several hockey teams and leagues formed. The local newspapers proclaimed, "Hockey will soon be the fashion. If you want to keep up with the times, play hockey."

In the fall of 1900, Canadian-born Jack "Doc" Gibson moved to Houghton and established a dental practice and in his first winter he joined the Portage Lake YMCA hockey team. Gibson was recognized as one of the best hockey players in Canada as he led the Portage Lake team to the Upper Peninsula Championship. Local interest grew as fans wanted to see Gibson and the team play. James Dee joined the Portage Lake team's executive board and the team started to recruit a few players from outside of the Copper Country for the second season. Gibson led the team to the Upper Peninsula

Championship again and they defeated a team from Chicago to be declared Champions of the West. In the summer of 1902, Dee organized a company to build a new arena on the Houghton waterfront to replace a smaller Palace Ice Rink. While the new arena was being built, Gibson was busy recruiting better players from Canada for the upcoming season. The Amphidrome opened on December 29, 1902 with a game between Portage Lake and the University of Toronto. The Portage Lake team was a good one that season and went undefeated and beat the Pittsburgh Bankers for the 1903 United States Championship.

In the fall of 1903, Gibson and Dee decided to recruit the best players from Canada and openly pay them to play for the Portage Lake hockey team—the first professional hockey team. The team had a good season and won the 1904 United States Championship again and defeated the Montreal Wanderers for what was billed as the World's Championship in March 1904. Following this successful season, Gibson and Dee began promoting the idea of a professional hockey league in which all of the players would be paid to play hockey, and in December 1904 play began in the International Hockey League (IHL). The league had five teams—Calumet, Pittsburgh, Portage Lake, Sault Ste. Marie Michigan, and Sault Ste. Marie Ontario, and although the league lasted only three seasons it was the start of professional hockey.

The book describes the events from when Gibson arrived in Houghton, the championships, and the formation and three seasons of the International Hockey League. Readers will learn more about hockey in that era, life in the Copper Country, other world events at the time, the five teams and communities, the players that played in the league, and what happened after the league folded. I have also introduced a few unique or interesting connections that readers may want to explore.

There are many that must be acknowledged for their contributions for this book project. Bernie Alkire, a colleague at Michigan Tech, suggested that I should volunteer to offer a hockey history course. The course was titled, "Hockey History and Culture" and quickly became a famous offering on campus and led me into an exciting area of hockey history research and discovery—thanks to every student who took the course and shared my passion for hockey. I sincerely thank Society for International Hockey Research (SIHR) members Bill Fitzell, Ernie Fitzsimmons, Roger Godin, James Milkes, Eric Zweig, and others who have always been so welcoming and willing to share their experiences and guidance for a hockey history book. Another SIHR member, Dan Mason wrote a thesis on the International Hockey League for a Master of Arts degree at the University of British Columbia almost twenty-five years ago. Dan and I became friends and continue to share information on the league. Local residents Scott MacInnes, Ralph Raffaelli, Bob Erkkila, John Haeussler, and Connie Julien have always been excited to hear about early hockey in the Copper Country and have been so willing to share photos and hockey stories and promote Houghton as the birthplace of professional hockey. Erik Nordberg, Lindsay Hiltunen, and the staff in the Michigan Tech University Library Archives, and Gloria Walli and Gerry Perrault of the Houghton County Historical Society Archives have all played invaluable roles in helping to find information and materials in their collections. I was also fortunate to meet two of "Doc" Gibson's grandsons, Jim and John Leech, who kindly shared materials and stories. Lloyd Wescoat, a colleague at Michigan Tech and owner of Grandpa's Barn bookstore in Copper Harbor, has always been a great source of encouragement and advice as I worked on the project, and Laura Smyth has been amazing in her roles in the editing and design process. Lastly, I am especially grateful to my wife, Hilary, and our sons, Davy and P.J., for their willingness to listen to my hockey stories and help whenever I needed it.

Bill Sproule
Houghton, Michigan

NO PLACE LIKE HOUGHTON
Copper Country Treats Athletes Better Than Other Sections

"If I were a great hockey player," said an old resident who is one of the puckeys, "I should certainly try and come to the Copper Country to play the game. No other part of the United States treats its athletes so well as the Copper Country. The people here treat the hockey players the best that men can be treated. They have the best of everything and so long as they do the right thing they are respected and supported as no other team ever was. I doubt if ever ten men in the country were the subject of such a celebration as occurred here last Saturday night and again Tuesday. The people would not have made any more stir had the President of the United States himself come to town. The same thing was true in the old baseball days. We had the best teams going and the people were crazy about them. Pittsburg hockey players go to the rink, play their game and go away again and nobody cares about them. They are just so many human machines so to speak who are set in motion to amuse the crowd for a brief space. If I were a hockey player I should certainly want to be a member of the Portage Lake team."

(Editorial in the *Houghton Daily Mining Gazette*, March 27, 1903 following the Portage Lake victory over the Pittsburg Bankers to win the 1903 United States championship.)

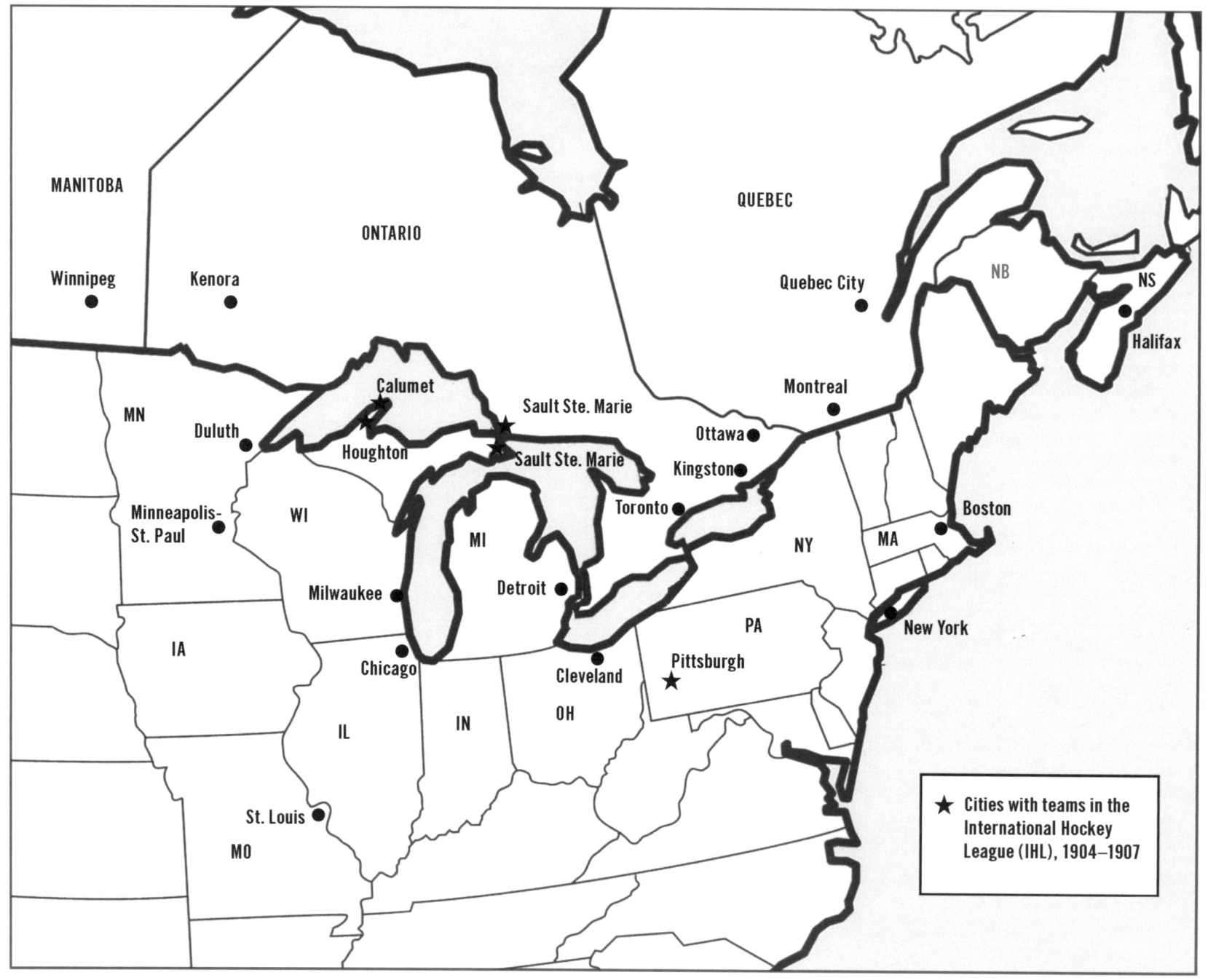

CHAPTER 1
Early Hockey History

FOR ALMOST AS LONG AS THE GAME OF ICE HOCKEY has existed, people have argued as to where the game was first played. Canadians will universally claim that hockey was born in Canada as after all it was in Canada where the sport grew, and it is where the sport has attained a religious-like following. Several communities including Montreal, Quebec; Windsor, Nova Scotia; Kingston, Ontario, and others have presented arguments as the birthplace of hockey in Canada.

However, it is very difficult to pinpoint the exact time and place that hockey began, as with any sport, the game has actually evolved. The earliest forms of hockey-like games were no doubt connected to the stick-and-ball games of brandy, field hockey, shinty, and hurley played in northern Europe and brought to Canada by immigrants as they settled in this new land. The early immigrants were probably introduced to lacrosse and other field games played by Canadian First Nations people so this new game of ice hockey was likely a blend of several games. Many of the early ice hockey games involved several players where rules were made at the start of a game. Today a popular term used for these unorganized games is "shinny" where the rules of play are adapted to the number of players, the size of the rink, how teams would be selected, and other aspects of a game.

James George Alwyn Creighton (Government of Canada Library and Archives)

Early Hockey in the Montreal Area

The earliest mention of an organized indoor game of hockey occurred at the Victoria Skating Rink in downtown Montreal on March 3, 1875 when James Creighton organized the first game as we might recognize it today. James George Alwyn Creighton was born in 1850 in Halifax, Nova Scotia. He inherited a passion for figure skating from his father and no doubt as young boy played shinny hockey on ponds in the Halifax area. Creighton graduated from Dalhousie University and worked on railroad projects in Nova Scotia before moving to Montreal to work as an engineer on several public works projects. Once in Montreal, Creighton joined the Victoria Skating Club and was welcomed as an expert figure skating judge. The Victoria Skating Club was in the center of Montreal's English community near McGill University and its members were among Montreal's upper class. Creighton organized early morning sessions at the Victoria Rink to introduce hockey to a few members of the Club and students from McGill University.

As this morning group became comfortable with the game, Creighton started to promote the idea of an exhibition game between two teams at the Victoria Rink and articles were published on hockey and rules for the upcoming game in the Montreal Gazette newspaper. Creighton used the rules of field hockey adapted for ice. The game was divided into two thirty-minute halves with nine men per side, and it introduced standardized goals, positions, referees, goal judges, and uniforms. One of the changes from field hockey was to replace the bouncing rubber ball with a flat circular piece of wood or puck to provide players with more control. It was less likely to bounce and injure spectators and break windows in the building. The event generated city-wide interest and the popularity of hockey grew quickly as several other teams formed in the community. Some additional work was completed on Creighton's informal rules and the first formal set of rules for ice hockey were published in the Montreal Gazette on February 27, 1877. These rules became known as the "Montreal Rules" or "McGill Rules," and although most of the original rules have changed over the years, scoring goals remains the objective. McGill established the first university hockey team in 1877 and within a few years there were several hockey teams and leagues in the Montreal and Quebec City area.

Creighton earned a law degree from McGill in 1880 and then practiced law with a Montreal law firm before he was offered a position in Ottawa as a law clerk to the Canadian Senate, a position that he would hold for almost 50 years. Ice hockey was becoming popular in the Ottawa area and several players who had learned the game in Montreal were being recruited for federal government civil service positions. Creighton moved to Ottawa and joined the new Rideau Skating and Curling Club and soon formed friendships with members of Parliament, Senators, their staffs, and the upper society of Ottawa.

Rules of Hockey 1877

The first rules of hockey were published in the February 27, 1877 edition of the *Montreal Gazette*. These rules, often referred to as the "Montreal Rules" or "McGill Rules," were similar to English field hockey rules of the era. A *bully* is a faceoff and a *puck* was used instead of a ball.

1. The game shall be commenced, and renewed by a bully from the center of the ground. Goals shall be changed after each game.

2. When a player hits the ball, any one of the same side who at such moment of hitting is nearer to the opponents' goal line is out of play, and may not touch the ball himself, or in any way whatever prevent any other player from doing so, until the ball has been played. A player must always be on his own side of the ball.

3. The ball may be stopped, but not carried or knocked on by any part of the body. No player shall raise his stick above his shoulder. Charging from behind, tripping, collaring, kicking, or shinning shall not be allowed.

4. When a ball is hit behind the goal line by the attacking side, it shall be bought out straight 15 yards, and started again by a bully; but, if hit behind by one of the side whose goal it is, a player of the opposite side shall hit it out from within one yard of the nearest corner, no player of the attacking side at that time shall be within 20 yards of the goal line, and the defenders, with the exception of the goal-keeper, must be behind their goal line.

5. When the ball goes off side, a player of the opposite side to that which hit it out shall roll it out from the point on the boundary line at which it went off at right angles with the boundary line, and shall not play it until it has been played by another player, every player being behind the ball.

6. On the infringement of any of the above rules, the ball shall be bought back and a bully shall take place.

7. All disputes shall be settled by the umpires, or in the event of their disagreement, by the referee.

From: *On His Own Side of the Puck—The Early History of Hockey Rules* by Iain Fyffe, Self Published, 2014.

The first hockey tournament was held on the St. Lawrence River as part of the 1883 Montreal Winter Carnival. The three team tournament included McGill University, a team from Quebec City, and another team from Montreal. Since the Quebec City team had only seven players, the Montreal teams agreed to play with seven instead of the traditional nine per side and this became the standard for almost thirty years. McGill University emerged as the tournament champion and the Montreal Carnival became the premier event to showcase ice hockey in Canada. In 1884 the tournament was held on the McGill campus and at the Victoria Skating Rink. The first hockey league, the Amateur Hockey Association of Canada (AHAC), was founded in 1886 with teams from Ottawa and Montreal (one from Ottawa and four from Montreal—McGill, the Victorias, the Crystals, and the Montreal Amateur Athletic Association), and competition rules were developed and they included specifications for a rubber vulcanized puck.

Lord Stanley and a Hockey Trophy

One of the most important figures of the early days of the game was a man who is never known to have skated, was not overly fond of cold weather, and who never saw a hockey game until his mid-forties. When Queen Victoria appointed Sir Frederick Arthur Stanley as the sixth Governor-General of Canada in June 1888, she never realized the significance of the appointment for hockey. It was a five year appointment as the Queen's official representative in Canada. Stanley was London-born and an avid sportsman and fisherman, but was virtually unaware of the new game of hockey played on ice in Canada. During the first winter after his arrival in Ottawa, Lord Stanley was invited to the 1889 Montreal Winter Carnival and among the events that he attended was a hockey game at the Victoria Rink. There was an outdoor rink on the grounds of Rideau Hall, his official residence in Ottawa, so skating and hockey became exciting pastimes. Stanley's daughter was one of the first women to play hockey. A local team called the Rideau Rebels included Stanley's two sons, Arthur and Edward, civil servants, Members of Parliament, and other members of Ottawa's high society. James Creighton and Philip Danken (P.D.) Ross were also members of the team. Ross was a McGill engineering graduate who had worked for newspapers in Montreal and Toronto prior to moving to Ottawa where he purchased the Ottawa Journal newspaper and became active in local politics.

The Rebels played exhibition games at the Rideau Club or on the outdoor rink at Rideau Hall. Although the games were serious sporting competitions, they were

A photograph of a hockey game at the Second Montreal Winter Carnival at McGill University in February 1884. This is believed to be the first photograph of a hockey game. (Government of Canada Library and Archives)

Sir Frederick Arthur Stanley—Lord Stanley (Government of Canada Library and Archives)

The 1889 Ottawa Rideau Rebels *were a recreational team of civil servants, aides, Senators, and members of the Canadian Parliament. The team hosted exhibition games in Ottawa and popularized the game in Ontario by touring the province. The team included James Creighton and two of Lord Stanley's sons—Arthur and Edward*

Standing, left to right: *Capt. Wingfield, Arthur Stanley, Senator L.G. Power, H.A. Ward, J. de St. D. Lemoine*
Seated, left to right: *Edward Stanley, James Creighton, Capt. A.H. MacMahon, John A. Barrow, Capt. H.B. Hawkes.* (Government of Canada Library and Archives)

Outdoor rink at Rideau Hall, the Governor General's official residence in Ottawa. The rink was popular for skating events and exhibition hockey games and it is believed that the first women's hockey game was played on this rink on March 8, 1889. Stanley's daughter, Isobel, played in the game. (Government of Canada Library and Archives)

also important social affairs and visiting teams were hosted to special lunches and dinners. The team would also travel for games in Montreal, Toronto, and other Ontario cities in the Governor-General's private rail car. A Toronto tour in February 1890 would have a major impact on hockey in Ontario. Following the tour, Arthur Stanley concluded that there was a need for a provincial organization to govern hockey in Ontario. At the time, numerous teams had been organized and they were playing "friendlies" or exhibition games on a challenge basis, however there was no organization to govern the game or declare a champion. Later that year, Stanley organized a meeting in Toronto and this meeting lead to the formation of the Ontario Hockey Association (OHA). The original executive committee included P.D. Ross and the committee wrote bylaws and basic playing rules for the Association. The OHA rules, with some variations, were adopted for use in Manitoba and western Canada as the game spread across the country.

An artist's painting of a hockey game between Montreal Victorias and Montreal AAA at the Victoria Skating Rink. (Government of Canada Library and Archives)

Ontario Hockey Association Rules of the Game, 1890

GAME

1. The game is played on ice by teams of seven on each side, with a puck made of vulcanized rubber, one inch thick all through and three inches in diameter.

The seven players would include a goalie, a point and cover point (similar to today's defensemen), three forwards (left wing, center, and right wing), and a rover.

STICKS

Hockey sticks shall not be more than three inches wide at any part, and not more than thirteen inches long in the blade.

GOAL

A goal is placed in the middle of each goal line, composed of two upright posts, four feet in height, placed six feet apart, and at least five feet from the end of the ice.

The goal posts shall be firmly fixed. In the event of a goal being displaced or broken, the Referee shall blow his whistle and the game shall not proceed until the post is replaced.

MATCH

2. Each side shall have a captain (a member of the team), who, before the match, shall toss for choice of goals.

3. Each side shall play on equal time from each end. The duration of championship matches shall not be less than one hour, exclusive of stoppages. The team scoring the greater number of goals in that time shall be declared the winner of the match. If at the end of that time the game is a draw, ends shall be changed and the game continued for ten minutes, each side playing five minutes from each end with a rest of five minutes between, and if neither side has scored a majority of games, similar periods of ten minutes shall be played in the same way until one side shall have scored a majority of goals.

TIME-KEEPERS

4. Time-keepers shall be appointed, one by each captain, to keep time during matches.

REFEREES

5. There shall be only one Referee for a match, and in no case shall he belong to either of the competing clubs. He shall enforce the rules, adjudicate upon disputes or cases unprovided for by rules; appoint the goal Umpires; control the Time-keepers; keep the score; and at the end match declare the result. The puck shall be considered in play until the Referee stops the game, which he may do at once when any irregularity of play occurs, by sounding a whistle. His decision shall be final.

In colder climates, the referee would often use a bell.

SCORE

6. A goal shall be scored when the puck shall have passed between the goal posts from in front and below an imaginary line drawn across the top of the posts.

GOAL UMPIRES

Goal Umpires shall inform the Referee when a goal is scored. Their decision shall be final.

FACE

7. The game shall be started and renewed by the Referee calling "play" after having placed the puck on its larger surface on the ice, between the sticks of two of the players, one from each team, who are to face it. After a goal has been scored the puck shall be played on the centre of the ice.

Today the face is known as a face off.

OFF-SIDE

8. A player shall always be on his side of the puck. A player is off-side when he is in front of the puck, or when the puck has been hit, touched or is being run with, by any of his own side behind him (i.e., between himself and the end of the rink near which his goal is placed).

A player being off-side is put on-side when the puck has been hit by, or touched the dress or person of any player of the opposite side, or when one of his own side has run in front of him, either with the puck or having played when behind him.

If a player when off-side plays the puck, or annoys or obstructs an opponent, the puck shall be faced where it was last played before the off-side play occurred.

KNOCKING-ON

9. The puck may not be stopped with the hand except by the goal keeper (see Rule 11) but may be stopped, but not carried, or knocked on by any other part of the body.

CHARGING, TRIPPING, ETC.

10. No player shall raise his stick above his shoulder. Charging from behind, tripping, collaring, kicking, cross-checking, or pushing shall not be allowed. And the Referee must rule off the ice, for any time in his discretion, a player who, in the opinion of the Referee, has deliberately offended against the above rule.

WHEN THE PUCK LEAVES THE ICE

11. When the puck goes off the ice behind the goal line it shall be bought out by the Referee to a point five yards in front of the goal line, on a line at right angles thereto, from the point at which it left the ice, and there faced.

When the puck goes off the ice at the side, it shall be similarly faced three yards from the side.

GOAL-KEEPER

12. The goal-keeper must not during play, lie, sit, or kneel upon the ice: he may, when in goal, stop the puck with his hands, but shall not throw or hold it. He may wear pads, but must not wear a garment such as would give him undue assistance in keeping goal. The Referee must rule off the ice, for any time in his discretion, a player who, in the opinion of the Referee, has offended deliberately against the rule.

CHANGE OF PLAYERS

13. No change of players shall be made after a match has commenced, except by reason of accident or injury during the game.

INJURED PLAYER

14. Should any player be injured during a match, break his skate, or from any other injury be compelled to leave the ice, the opposite side shall immediately drop a man to equalize the teams. In the event of any dispute, the matter shall at once be decided by the Referee.

STOPPAGES

15. Should the game be stopped by the Referee by reason of infringement of any of the rules, or because of an accident or change of players, the puck shall be faced at the spot where it was last played, before such infringement, accident or change of players shall have occurred.

From, *Hockey: Canada's Royal Winter Game—Handbook* by Arthur Farrell, 1899.

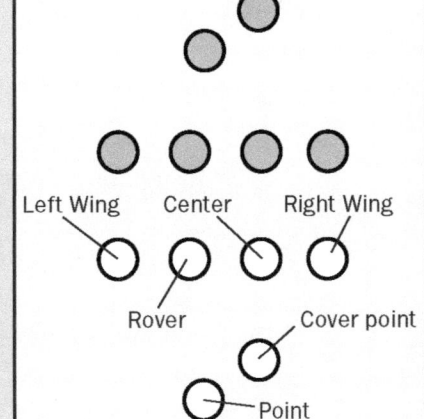

Early Hockey Positions
Early hockey teams had seven players—goalkeeper (goalie), point, cover point, left wing, center, right wing, and rover. The position of rover was eliminated in 1911, and the point and cover point eventually became known as defense.

In the first season (1890–91), the Ontario Hockey Association had thirteen senior teams from Toronto, Kingston, Ottawa, and Lindsay in which they would play a series of elimination games leading to a single championship game. The team from Ottawa, led by its captain P.D. Ross, defeated a Toronto team for the first OHA championship. That same year the University of Toronto started a hockey team and they were soon playing teams from McGill University and Queen's University. The Ottawa hockey club won the OHA senior championship again in 1892. Lord Stanley followed the team and attended many of their games and at a celebration banquet on March 18, 1892 to honor the success of the Ottawa club, Lord Kilcoursie, Stanley's aide-de-camp, announced that the Governor General wished to donate a hockey trophy for the best team in Canada.

"I have for some time been thinking that it would be a good thing if there were a challenge cup which would be held from year to year by the champion hockey club in the Dominion (of Canada). Considering the general interest which hockey now elicits, and the importance of having the game played fairly and under rules generally recognized, I am willing to give a cup which shall be held from year to year by the winning club."

Stanley directed another aid to travel to England to purchase a silver bowl for ten guineas (about $50 at the time). He had the words, "Dominion Hockey Challenge Cup" engraved on one side of the bowl and "From Stanley of Preston" on the other. Stanley intended that the Cup be awarded to the top amateur hockey team in Canada, to be decided by the acceptance of a challenge from another team. He appointed two trustees and made the following provisions:

- The winners shall return the Cup in good order when required by the trustees so that it may be handed over to any other team which may win it.
- Each winning team, at its expense, may have the club name and year engraved on a silver ring fitted on the Cup.
- The Cup shall remain a challenge cup, and should not become the property of one team, even if won more than one time.
- The trustees shall remain absolute authority in all situations or disputes over the winner of the Cup.
- If one of the existing trustees resigns, the remaining trustee shall nominate a substitute.

The first trustees were John Sweetland, a medical doctor and Ottawa sheriff, and P.D. Ross. Although Stanley did not want the trophy to be named after him, the trophy soon became known as the "Stanley Cup." The Cup was first presented in 1893 to the Montreal Hockey Club of the Montreal Amateur Athletic Association, champions of the Amateur Hockey Association of Canada (AHAC), however the decision to award the Cup to Montreal was controversial so the trustees issued more specific rules on how the trophy should be defended and awarded:

- Challenges for the Cup must be from teams from senior hockey associations, and they must have won their league championship. Challengers will be recognized in the order in which their request is received.
- The challenge games are to be decided either in one-game, a two-game total goals, or a best of three series. All matches are to take place on the home ice of the champions, although specific dates and times have to be approved by the trustees.
- Ticket receipts from the challenge games are to be split equally between the two teams.
- If the two competing clubs cannot agree to a referee, the trustees will appoint one, and the two teams will cover the expenses equally.
- A league cannot challenge for the Cup twice in one season.

The 1893 Montreal Amateur Athletic Association hockey team—*the first winner of the Stanley Cup (Note the original Stanley Cup in the photograph).* (Government of Canada Library and Archives)

Standing, left to right: *Alex Irving, Haviland Routh, Allan Cameron*
Seated, left to right: *Harry Shaw, George Lowe, Tom Paton, James Stewart, Archie Hodgson, Alex Kingan, Billy Barlow*
Trophies: *1885 Montreal Winter Carnival Trophy (Birks Cup), AHAC Trophy, Stanley Cup, 1887 Montreal Winter Carnival Trophy (Birks Cup)*

Stanley never saw a Cup championship game as he returned to England when his term ended in September 1893. There are many stories of early Cup challenges and one of the most famous challenges was from Dawson City, Yukon. In the early days of the Stanley Cup a team could win the Cup in two different ways—by winning the league championship in which the defending Cup holder played, or by issuing a challenge to the current Cup holder and defeating them. In the summer of 1904, a challenge came from Joe Boyle, a Toronto-born prospector and investor who had struck it rich in the 1898 Yukon Gold Rush. He recruited the best players from Dawson City and wanted to play the Ottawa Silver Seven, the current holders of the Stanley Cup. The two-game challenge was accepted by the trustees and the first game was scheduled to be played in Ottawa on Friday, January 13, 1905. The travel plans for the 4,000 mile trip were daunting. The team would bicycle and dog sled from Dawson City to Whitehouse where they would board a train to Skagway, Alaska. From there they traveled by steamship to Vancouver to board a train for the cross Canada journey. Canadian newspapers followed them as they traveled across Canada and they tried to recruit better players to join the team. As the team traveled through Manitoba, one player that they sought was Fred Taylor but he declined and a few weeks later he signed a professional contract to play for Portage Lake in the International Hockey League. The team arrived in Ottawa after a twenty-five day ordeal and with only one day rest they played the Ottawa Silver Seven. Before a sold-out crowd

Dawson City Nuggets *played in the Stanley Cup Challenge Series of January 1905 in Ottawa against the Ottawa Silver Seven.* (Yukon Archives)
Standing, left to right: *Hector Smith (forward), George "Sureshot" Kennedy (forward), Lorne Hannay (cover point), Jim Johnstone (point), Norman Watt (forward)*
Seated, left to right: *Albert Forrest (goal)*, Joe Boyle (manager), Dr. Randy McLennan (rover)*
*Forrest was 17 years old and is the youngest player to ever play in a Stanley Cup game

1905 Ottawa Silver Seven (Government of Canada Library and Archives)
Standing, left to right: *Harry Westwick (rover), Mac McGilton (trainer), Billy Gilmour (forward), Frank McGee (forward)***
Seated, left to right: *Dave Finnie (goal), Harvey Pulford (point), Alf Smith (forward), Arthur Moore (cover point)*
**McGee holds the record of 14 goals scored in a Stanley Cup game as Ottawa defeated Dawson City 23-2 in the second game of the two-game series

at the Dey's Rink the talent gap between the two teams was apparent. Ottawa defeated Dawson City 9-2. Boyle was optimistic and had to regroup quickly for the second game the next night. The Ottawa team beat Dawson City 23-2 and the game was called early; Frank McGee scored a Stanley Cup record fourteen goals. Dawson City continued their barnstorming tour with games in the Maritimes, Quebec, Ontario, and Manitoba. They also played in Pittsburgh and exhibition games were proposed in Calumet but the arrangements could not be finalized. The exhausted team returned to Dawson City in early April 1905 after the four month road trip. Following this series, the Stanley Cup trustees tighten the rules for future challenges.

Amateur Hockey in Canada

In the early years hockey was considered to be a gentleman's sport and strictly an "amateur" game primarily for the English-speaking upper class of society. The "amateur ideal" was a core component of Canadian sporting tradition that began as a way of keeping the working-class people out of sports leagues. Teams were organized by exclusive men's athletic clubs or organizations and universities, and club members paid fees to support their teams. But as hockey grew it became extremely popular among all social classes and players developed in large cities and small towns throughout Canada.

For some, hockey was just a game, but for others it was an opportunity to make money. Better facilities for players and spectators were built in the larger cities and competition between clubs, leagues, and cities created a demand for the best players. Teams would recruit players from across all social classes and although all players were amateurs, teams found numerous ways to provide remuneration to the best players—gold watches, diamond rings, or new skates, and players would have their medical expenses covered, stay at the best hotels, and eat in the finest restaurants. Some teams would recruit players by arranging attractive employment in their town or city.

Hockey became a lucrative game for "amateur" athletic clubs and they began to negotiate the sharing of gate revenues and travel

Hockey players on an outdoor rink in Montreal in the early 1900s (Government of Canada Library and Archives)

expenses. Games were promoted and advertised extensively in newspapers to attract spectators. Gambling was also a source of revenue with owners, players, and fans alike betting. However despite all of the money coming from hockey none was going to the players.

By mid-1890s, there were rumors that ice hockey players were actually paid to play and this became quite controversial in Canada. Hockey organizations were formed to foster amateur hockey in Canada and protect it from professionalism. The most powerful hockey organization in Canada was the Ontario Hockey Association (OHA) and the threat of professionalism became a main concern in which they would investigate any hint of players being paid to play hockey. In the late 1890s and early 1900s the OHA was led by John Ross Robertson, a powerful Toronto businessman and philanthropist who owned the Toronto Telegram newspaper, and his anti-professionalism stance shaped hockey during this era in which several top players were suspended or banned under the suspicion of accepting money to play hockey.

The Ontario Hockey Association was founded in 1890 with one league of senior men's hockey. In 1892 a junior division was introduced for competition at a lower level and then in 1897 an intermediate division was established for teams from small Ontario towns. A team from Berlin (now Kitchener) and Waterloo defeated the Kingston Frontenacs for the first intermediate championship and among the members of the Berlin-Waterloo team were Edward and Joseph Seagram, from the famous Seagram distillery family, and Jack Gibson. Gibson would eventually play an important role in Houghton hockey history. In the following year, Berlin formed a separate team and in an early season game it defeated crosstown rival Waterloo. Oscar Rumpel, Mayor of Berlin and manager of the team, was so elated over the victory that he ran onto the ice at the end of the game and presented $10 gold coins to each Berlin player. The Ontario Hockey Association heard about the incident and expelled the team and declared the players to be professionals. The suspension was lifted at the end of the season, but the ruling would change hockey in the years that followed. Among the team members were Jack Gibson and Art Farrell. Farrell would go on to write the first book on ice hockey, *Hockey: Canada's Royal Winter Game* in 1899, which included a section on the history of hockey and explained how to play the game. He also wrote two how-to-play hockey books (*Ice Hockey and Ice Polo Guide*, and *How to Play Hockey*) for the Spalding Sports Series. Farrell played four seasons for the Montreal Shamrocks in the Canadian Amateur Hockey League but died from tuberculosis at the age of 32. He was inducted into the Hockey Hall of Fame in 1965.

1897 Berlin-Waterloo Hockey Club—*the first OHA Intermediate Champion* (City of Kitchener)
Standing, left to right: *L.Hueglin (trainer), Joe Seagram (cover point), Jack Gibson (point), Carlo Boehmer (goal)*
Seated, left to right: *Peter Livingston (forward), Ed Seagram (forward), F.G. Oliver (manager), W.H. Dixon (forward), J.A. MacDonald (forward)*

1898 Berlin Hockey Club (City of Kitchener)
Standing, left to right: *C. Meinke (trainer), P. Robson (forward), Jack Gibson (point), F. Stephens (cover point)*
Seated, left to right: *Art Farrell (forward), C. H. Boehmer (goal), W. Rumpel (assistant manager), O. Rumpel (manager), F. Clark (forward), J.A. MacDonald (forward)*

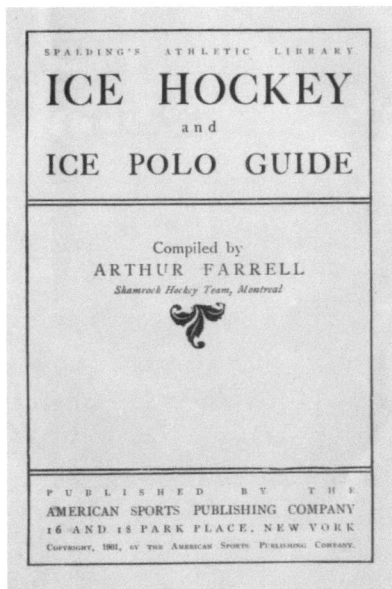

Spaldings Ice Hockey and Ice Polo Guide from 1901. (Spalding)

Arthur Farrell (Government of Canada Library and Archives)

Development of Hockey in the United States

Hockey had a different evolution in the United States as it developed out of the roller skating craze of the 1870s. Roller skating became a popular activity and entrepreneurs and private associations built roller rinks as both men and women learned to roller skate. But skating lap after lap was often boring so "fancy" skating was introduced as skaters learned to perform loops and jumps for shows and competitions. Others sought to adapt other sports to roller versions. An exciting game called "roller polo" caught on quickly in the 1880s as local polo teams and leagues, affiliated with roller rinks, were organized in New England and the Midwest. Roller rinks would be adapted with boards and goal nets (called cages) and teams of five to seven players would play three 15-minute innings (periods) for a game. The rules were similar to field hockey and players would use sticks similar to field hockey sticks and would use one hand to hold their stick. Games started when a bright colored rubber ball was dropped at the center of the rink and the forwards would sprint from the ends of the rink and battle for the ball. The wave of roller rink development continued through the decade but the interest in roller skating and roller polo began to decline in the 1890s. As roller polo faded some players moved on to the ice with a game called "ice polo." Ice polo adopted roller polo rules but players would wear ice skates and the game grew quickly in New England, Minnesota, and Michigan's Upper Peninsula where games were played on outdoor rinks or on indoor skating rinks.

Artist's sketch of a roller polo game—illustration by C.W. Weldon in Harper's Weekly, *September 8, 1882*

A New England ice polo team of 1890s (Library of Congress)

Arthur McSwigan (University of Pittsburgh Library and Archives)

Ice hockey was introduced in the United States in the mid-1890s as teams from Montreal and Ottawa would travel to New York and other New England cities to play men's athletic and university clubs, and teams from Winnipeg would travel to the Minneapolis-St. Paul area. When Canadian teams traveled to the United States they would usually play one match using ice polo rules and one match with ice hockey rules. However, shortly after these exhibition contests ice hockey was viewed to be more exciting and soon replaced ice polo. Amateur hockey leagues formed in New York, New England, and Minnesota, and an intercollegiate hockey league of Ivy League schools was organized within a few years. Indoor arenas were built to accommodate large crowds and artificial ice technology made hockey attractive in several larger U.S. cities.

Another region in the United States where ice hockey became very popular in the 1890s was Pittsburgh. In 1893 James Conat convinced Pittsburgh investors to build a new entertainment complex "for people of stature and the common man" that would include a grand theater and an indoor artificial ice skating surface. The new Schenley Park Casino opened in 1895 and it was the envy of the entertainment industry. Conat was hired to manage the complex and he had heard about ice hockey through fellow amusement promoters involved with traveling ice skating demonstrations. He felt that hockey exhibitions would captivate the interest of Casino patrons so he recruited teams from Canada to demonstrate this new game. Queen's University was one of the first teams to introduce the game in Pittsburgh in December 1895. Ice hockey was extremely well received and other Canadian teams traveled to Pittsburgh and Conant organized local hockey leagues. Unfortunately, the Casino burned in just the second season but soon others in the community began thinking about a replacement. Local

Program for the winter season at the Duquesne Garden (University of Pittsburgh Library and Archives)

The Duquesne Gardens in Pittsburgh's Oakland neighborhood. (University of Pittsburgh Library and Archives)

Photograph of a game between the Pittsburgh Athletic Club and Queen's University in Duquesne Gardens, January 1901. The Duquesne Gardens had an artificial ice surface and a seating capacity for 5,000 spectators. (University of Pittsburgh Library and Archives)

investors, led by Christopher Magee, purchased the old Duquesne Traction Company streetcar barn, renovated it, and renamed the structure the Duquesne Gardens, although locals always called it the Arena. Magee hired Conant to be its manager and the Gardens opened in January 1899. Ice hockey returned to Pittsburgh with teams competing in local leagues and Conant and another local hockey promoter, Arthur McSwigan, began to explore the idea of recruited Canadian players for a new league. They formally established the Western Pennsylvania Hockey League (WPHL) with three teams—the Pittsburgh Athletic Club, the Pittsburgh Bankers, and the Pittsburgh Keystones, and play began with the 1901–02 season. A fourth team, the Pittsburgh Victorias, joined the league in the next season. The four teams lured players from Canada with promises of high-paid employment and small cash incentives of $10 to $15 per week. The teams were supported by local businesses and organizations and the team manager would be given a lump sum to pay players, but the less money that the manager had to pay the players, the more money that the manager got to keep. In spite of the apparent pay, the League was considered to an amateur league as teams played exhibition games against Canadian teams. The Ontario Hockey Association was always watchful and would ban players or teams who played for money. Any player questioned about being paid to play hockey would deny the accusation and say that they moved to Pittsburgh for a job and played hockey for fun.

By 1900 sport was no longer a privilege of affluent members of society and this made regulation by the different operators of the sporting clubs and amateur bodies increasingly difficult. As the century ended, amateur status was no longer determined by social position and a player was declared professional based on the monetary rewards received for his athletic performance. By the beginning of the twentieth century, hockey had evolved into a sport with standardized rules, equipment, and facilities.

CHAPTER 2
Houghton and the Copper Country

HOUGHTON IS LOCATED IN HOUGHTON COUNTY ON the Keweenaw Peninsula in Michigan's Upper Peninsula. The area is known as the Copper Country due to its rich history of copper mining.

The First Mining Boom in the United States

When the Michigan Territory was established in 1805, it included only the Lower Peninsula and the eastern portion of the Upper Peninsula. As Michigan was preparing for statehood in the 1830s, several proposals for boundaries left out the Upper Peninsula and there was a border dispute with Ohio. In 1837, a compromise was reached in which the coveted Toledo Strip would be part of Ohio and the Upper Peninsula would become part of the state of Michigan. At that time, Michiganders felt that they had been cheated in the trade, but this opinion soon changed when rich mineral deposits were discovered. Douglass Houghton, the official geologist of the newly formed state of Michigan, reported on the prospects for copper mining in the Keweenaw Peninsula to the state legislature in 1841 and his report sparked a rush of adventurers and investors hoping to become rich—it was also the first U.S. mining boom, preceding the famous California Gold Rush. While many of the early mines failed, a few were successful, and eventually several major mining companies formed. Boom towns sprang up across the area. From the Civil War to the turn of the 20th century, the Upper Peninsula alone produced more copper, iron ore, and lumber than any other state in the Union. The center of copper mining was the Keweenaw Peninsula, a strip of land jutting into Lake Superior, and during this era, over 80 percent of the nation's copper was produced in the region that became known

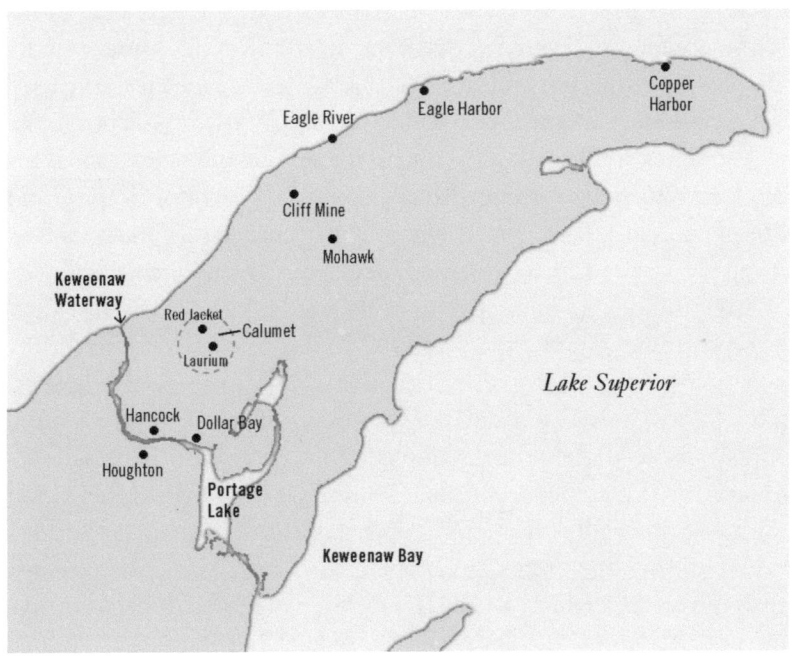

as the "Copper Country." When Horace Greeley made the famous statement, "Go West, Young Man" he was not speaking of the western United States but rather Michigan's western Upper Peninsula.

The initial copper mining boom was in the Copper Harbor, Eagle Harbor, and Eagle River areas on the north end of the peninsula. In 1849, the Cliff Mine opened near the present day Eagle River, and paid large returns to the original investors, many of whom were from the Boston and New York area. A few years later, C.C. Douglas discovered copper just north of Portage Lake and this discovery launched the Quincy Mining Company. As the Cliff mines were approaching exhaustion, a major copper discovery in Calumet Township was made in 1858 by Edwin Hubert while he was surveying for a road. He shipped a barrel of copper conglomerate to Boston to convince investors of his discovery and in 1864 he formed two mining companies—the Calumet Mining Company and the Hecla Mining Company. However, one of Hubert's financial backers from Boston was Quincy Shaw and he soon became critical of Hubert and asked his brother-in-law, Alexander Agassiz, to take over the operations of the companies. Under Agassiz's management the mines rapidly increased production and in 1871 the two companies were merged to become the Calumet and Hecla Mining Company (C&H). Agassiz became President of the company and he would serve until his death in 1910 and was succeeded by James MacNaughton as the C&H President. The C&H was the region's most successful copper mining company. Over its history shareholders were paid dividends in excess of $160 million and employment peaked at 11,000.

The mining companies required a large workforce and they recruited men and provided them and their families with houses, schools, hospitals, and libraries. They donated land for churches and parks and encouraged the development of shops and other businesses to serve their employees and their families. The village of Red Jacket was the community that sprang up adjacent to Calumet and Hecla's initial mining operations in Calumet Township. Red Jacket became the commercial center of the area. The village of Red Jacket was incorporated in 1875. As other mines opened, housing was developed

The copper mines provided employment for thousands of workers from around the world who came to seek their fortune in the Copper Country. (Michigan Technological University Archives and Copper Country Historical Collections)

in such locations as Blue Jacket, Yellow Jacket, Raymbaultown, Swedetown, Albion, and Laurium. Laurium was located southeast of Red Jacket and it was originally platted and known as the village of Calumet. In 1895 the residents of the community wanted their own post office but the Red Jacket post office was named Calumet so they changed the name of the community to the village of Laurium. Laurium became the residential area with many large homes and mansions for merchants, bankers, mining managers and executives. Red Jacket was officially renamed "Calumet" in 1929.

The Keweenaw Waterway cuts across the south end of the Keweenaw Peninsula and connects to Lake Superior at the north and south entries. Portage Lake is part of the Keweenaw waterway system. Hancock is located on the north side of the waterway and Houghton is on the south side. In the 1860s, in a joint venture between the United States government and several mining companies, the waterway was dredged and a canal was constructed that would allow ships to haul copper from the mines on the Peninsula

The center of copper mining was the Calumet area. The largest mining company was Calumet and Hecla, and part of its operations can be seen in the distance. (Library of Congress Detroit Publishing Collection)

One of the Calumet and Hecla smelter operations is shown in this photograph. (Michigan Technological University Archives and Copper Country Historical Collections)

through the new Soo Locks to markets in Detroit and Chicago. The waterway would also enable ships to bring supplies to the region and provided safe settler for ships crossing Lake Superior during stormy conditions. As mines opened in the south end of the peninsula, Hancock and Houghton became transportation gateways as well as commercial centers.

The initial settlements in Hancock and Houghton occurred in the 1850s and ferry service linking the two communities was established. Houghton was incorporated as a village in 1861 and the village of Hancock was incorporated in 1875. In 1876, the Portage Lake Bridge Company built a wooden toll bridge across the waterway for foot and wagon traffic and then in 1897, a replacement bridge, constructed of steel, opened.

The mining wealth led to the development of rail lines which linked communities in the Copper Country and connected the region to the outside world. The first passenger and freight railroad opened between Hancock and the Calumet area in 1873, and rail service between Houghton and Marquette began in 1883. When the new bridge opened with railroad tracks on the lower level rail service was then available between Houghton and the Calumet area with links to the Duluth, South Shore, and Atlantic Railroad and the Chicago, Milwaukee, and St. Paul Railroad. By 1900, the Copper Country had several passenger and freight railroad alternatives to reach anywhere in the United States and Canada. Streetcar service began in 1900 with the opening of a line between Houghton, Hancock, and Boston with extensions to Red Jacket and Laurium (Calumet area), Wolverine, Mohawk, Lake Linden, and Hubbell in subsequent years. The streetcar provided frequent and relatively inexpensive transportation that soon became extremely popular for travel between Copper Country communities.

As the mines developed, thousands of Americans and immigrants moved to the area. The first wave were the Cornish from England, followed by Irish, Germans, and Canadians, and then in the 1890s, Finnish immigrants began settling in large numbers. Mining was tough work and dangerous and an average miner worked sixty hours

Houghton Waterfront—late 1800s with the original bridge between Houghton and Hancock. Houghton was the transportation gateway to the Copper Country with rail connections and shipping docks. (Michigan Technological University Archives and Copper Country Historical Collections)

Photograph of the new bridge linking Houghton and Hancock in early 1900s. The Lake Superior Smelting Company is located in the foreground of the photograph, and the Copper Range Railroad Houghton depot is located on the south end of the bridge, on the right. The bridge had two levels—the lower level was for intercity passenger and freight trains, the upper level for streetcars, carriages, and vehicles. (Michigan Technological University Archives and Copper Country Historical Collections)

Railroads were the primary mode of transportation linking the Copper Country with areas to the south. The Copper Range Railroad; the Duluth, South Shore, and Atlantic Railroad (DSS&A); and the Mineral Range Railroad (a subsidiary of the DSS&A) provided daily passenger and freight services on several trains. (Michigan Technological University Archives and Copper Country Historical Collections)

CHAPTER 2: HOUGHTON AND THE COPPER COUNTRY ● 31

Streetcar service began in 1900 and provided frequent service linking several communities in the Copper Country. Note the advertisement for hockey on the car on the left. (Michigan Technological University Archives and Copper Country Historical Collections)

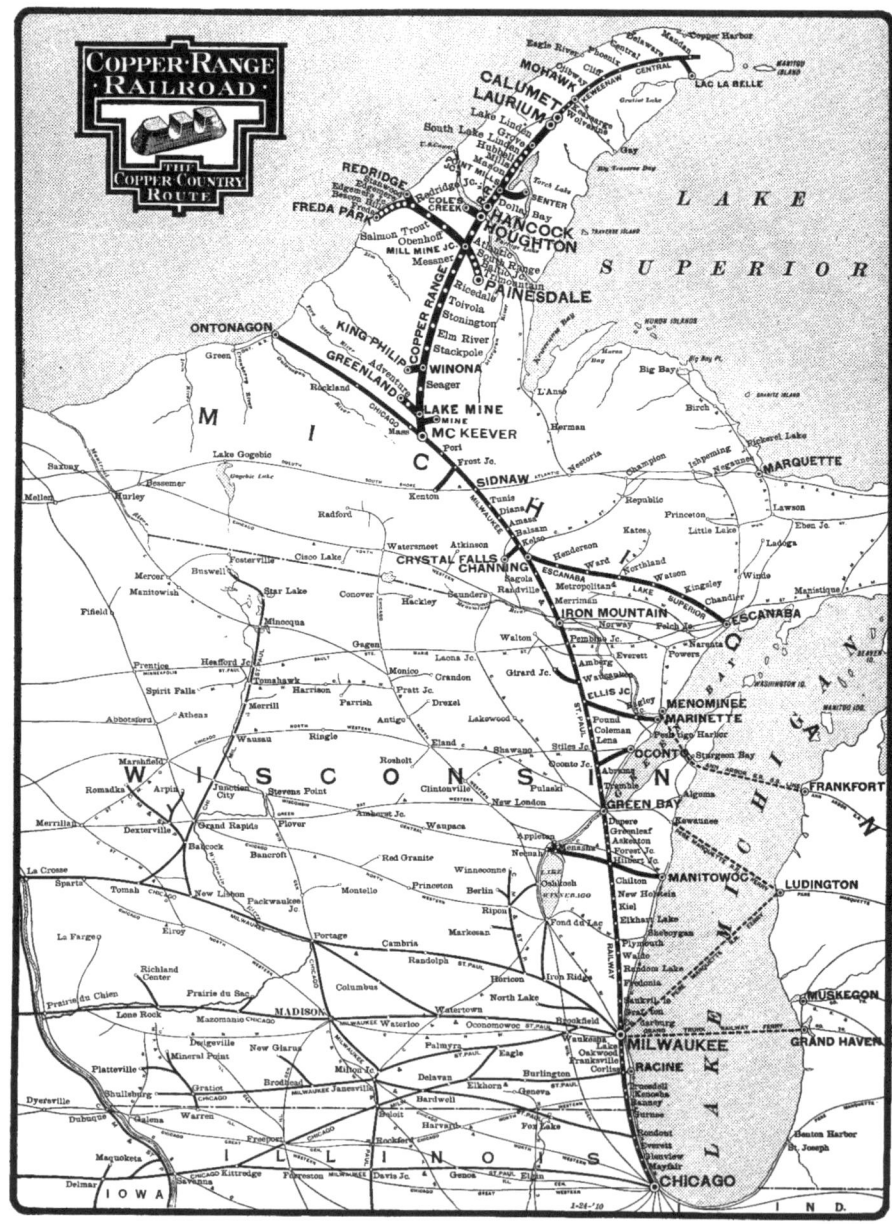

There were several railroads in Michigan's Upper Peninsula with numerous connections. Chicago was probably the most common destination for passenger travel. (Michigan Technological University Archives and Copper Country Historical Collections)

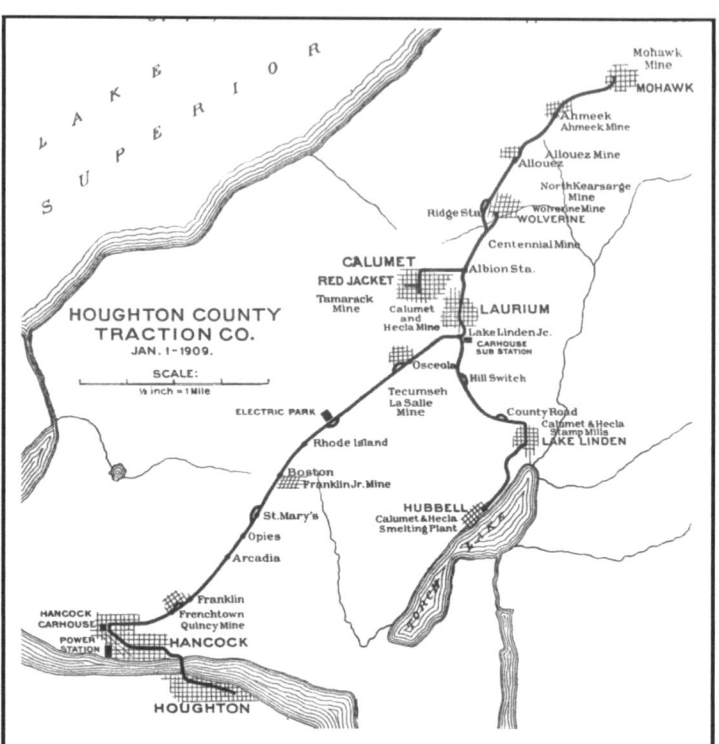

A 1909 map that shows the route and stations on the Houghton County Traction Company streetcar system. Service began between Houghton and Boston on October 27, 1900. In 1901, the line was extended farther north to serve Laurium, Red Jacket, and Wolverine, and in 1903, a branch line opened to Lake Linden and Hubbell. The network was completed when the section between Wolverine and Mohawk opened in 1908. The streetcars operated in the Copper Country until 1932. (Michigan Technological University Archives and Copper Country Historical Collections)

a week in ten hour shifts, six days a week. While many were first drawn to work in the mines many immigrants found ways to return to more traditional occupations in business and services in the local communities. French Canadians were attracted to the Upper Peninsula and the Copper Country for logging and lumber mills. It is hard to imagine today, but in the early 1900s ten intercity trains arrived in the Copper Country every day, there were over twenty newspapers in four languages, and residents could attend events at one of seven theaters and two opera houses that attracted such luminaries as John Phillip Sousa, actor Douglas Fairbanks, actress Sarah Bernhardt, and escapist Henri Houdini. The Copper Country was as cosmopolitan as New York or Boston. The area had over thirty churches, thirty schools, hundreds of saloons and bars, and numerous men's fraternal organizations, ethnic clubs, and brothels.

At the turn of the century the Copper Country was the most prosperous area in the world due to the demand for copper as the electrical industry grew. Houghton County had more millionaires per capita than any other county in the United States. The 1900 census recorded the population of the county at over 66,000 with 26,000 in the Calumet area, 3,500 in Houghton, and 4,000 in Hancock. The county also had the largest Chinese, Italian, Finnish, Slovenia, and Croatian communities in Michigan. Houghton County grew to almost 100,000 in the decade and over 88,000 residents were recorded in the 1910 census. In 1900, the population of both Marquette and Sault Ste. Marie, Michigan was about 10,000 and over 50,000 lived in Duluth. Minneapolis-St. Paul was over 350,000 while Detroit was almost 300,000 but it experienced amazing growth over the next twenty-five years as the automobile industry developed. Chicago, with a population of over 1.7 million, was the center for business activity and rail travel for the Copper Country during this era.

Early Sports in the Copper Country

The mining companies supported athletics and often set aside a portion of their lands for sports fields. In the winter, the companies flooded open ground to create skating rinks and many residents would build ice rinks in their backyard or neighborhood or they would skate on Portage Lake. In the 1880s, skating was a popular winter activity and skating races were common. Top racers from the across the U.S. would travel to the area to skate exhibitions and compete against local racers. About this time, roller skating was also gaining popularity in many parts of the United States and from this came the game of roller polo. Indoor rinks were built for roller skating and roller polo and several polo leagues formed. There was a summer roller polo league in the Upper Peninsula with teams from Calumet, Escanaba, Houghton, Marquette, and Negaunee and in fact, Houghton won the league's championship in 1885.

Houghton Roller Polo team—*1885 Upper Peninsula Champions* Standing, left to right: *Louis Krellwitz, Robert Haas, John Schults. Seated, left to right: Martin Hoar, Harry Major, Joseph Sewell, Pat Sauce* (Houghton County Historical Society)

34 ● HOUGHTON: THE BIRTHPLACE OF PROFESSIONAL HOCKEY

Skating was very popular in the Copper Country and here skaters and hockey players enjoy Portage Lake.

(Michigan Technological University Archives and Copper Country Historical Collections)

In the late 1880s, roller polo evolved into the winter sport of ice polo and games were played on outdoor or indoor ice skating rinks. Ice polo became very popular in eastern Canada, New England, Minnesota, and the Copper Country, but by the end of the 1890s the interest in ice polo declined and was replaced by the winter sport of ice hockey. There were several skating rinks in the Copper Country during this period including a rink in Dollar Bay, the Superior Ice Rink in Laurium, and the Mammoth Skating Rink in Lake Linden. The Mammoth Rink was the home to many of the local ice polo games at the time.

Baseball was the popular summer sport in the Copper Country as local community teams played in numerous leagues and the best teams would travel to play other teams in the Upper Peninsula. In the early 1900s, there were semi-professional baseball teams in the Copper Country that would compete against teams from Duluth, Marquette, Sault Ste. Marie, Winnipeg, and other communities, and salaries of up to $225 per month would be paid to baseball players to come to this isolated area.

> One week from Wednesday, two hockey teams from Dollar Bay will go to Calumet, where they will give an exhibition game to give the skaters there an idea as to how to play the game. A team has already been organized at Dollar Bay and much interest is taken in the game. An exhibition game will also be played at the Hancock ring as soon as it is completed. It is the intention of the Dollar Bay aggregation to work up interest in the game and have teams organized in the different towns in the county, and it is thought that a tournament being held will be the outcome.

Newspaper clipping from Copper Country Evening News, *Dec. 1897.*

Ice Hockey Introduced in the Copper Country

The first stories of ice hockey in the Copper Country date back to the winter of 1897, when a team was organized by Ernest Yates in Dollar Bay. Yates was born and raised in Canada and worked as a machinist for the Hancock Chemical Company, a company that manufactured explosives for use in the mining industry. When Yates moved to the area he brought a passion for hockey and organized a team of fellow Canadians and workers, and for those new to ice hockey he taught the fundamentals of the game. Among the members of the team were Ernest Yates as captain, his brother Harry Yates, Ned Rogers, Grif Williams, Herman Rosberg, and Frank Frenette, and during this first winter they practiced and played a couple of exhibition contests with a team from Marquette. In the following season several contests were played in the Copper Country and the press would refer to the Dollar Bay team as the "Pioneers."

On December 29, 1897, two teams from Dollar Bay played an exhibition of ice hockey at an outdoor rink in Red Jacket. It was Yates's intention to generate interest and have teams organize in the different towns in the county. Under the headline, "The Game of Hockey Introduced Last Evening," the Copper Country Evening News reported that the game made a favorable impression and it was more than likely that a team would be organized by local skaters. A week later the two Dollar Bay teams played another exhibition at the new Twin City ice rink in Ripley. From the newspaper reports the attendance was rather small and not what it should have been as the game deserves the support of the people and should be a characteristic sport of the Upper Peninsula. On the other hand the conditions were not favorable as the ice was soft and the posts down the center of the rink bothered the players. However the teams put up a good game and gave a good exhibition of the sport. As with most spectator events of that era, the

> **The Game of Hockey Introduced Last Evening.**
>
> **Two Teams From Dollar Bay**
>
> Participate In the Exciting Game—Davey And Gilmore to Race at the Superior Rink.
>
> The attendance at the Skating Pavilion last evening was the largest it has been this winter. The game of hockey between the Reds and Whites, the two crack teams of Dollar Bay, proved most interesting. The teams were rather late in arriving and the game did not come off until 10 o'clock. It was a close contest and proved as interesting for the spectators as it was exciting for the participants. The game resulted in a draw neither side being able to score against the other. The game made a most favorable impression here and it is more than likely that a team will shortly be organized among local skaters. It is as fully exciting and gives just as many opportunities for the players to show their skill as polo and is still lacking of the rough features which usually characterize polo. The pavilion will be open every afternoon and evening for the remainder of the week with the Fifth Regiment band present Saturday evening. The band was in attendance last evening and rendered some of their choicest selections.

Newspaper clippings from the Copper Country Evening News, *December 30, 1897.*

> The Twin City ice rink will be open every afternoon from 2:20 until 5:30 o'clock to give beginners an opportunity of learning the art of skating. Instructors will be furnished those who need them.

> A match game of hockey between the Dollar Bay and Woodside teams is advertised to be played tonight at the Twin City rink. The Quincy Excelsior band is advertised to furnish music for dancing and skating. The game will be called at 8 o'clock.

> Considerable interest is being taken in the new game of hockey by Portage Lake skaters. A team has been organized by some of the Mining school boys and another team has been gotten up at the smelting works. After a few practice games have been played the teams will come together in a game to be played at the Twin City ice rink. There is good material in both teams and it will be a hard fought contest. When the boys are all in trim the Dollar Bay team will have to look to their laurels.

Newspaper clippings from the Copper Country Evening News *from January 1898.*

Quincy Excelsior Band was on hand to liven things up. Quoting from the newspaper account of the game, "The game is somewhat similar to polo but not nearly as exciting and it is feared very little interest will be taken in the game by our head skaters." (Copper Country Evening News, January 10, 1898)

Fortunately, ice hockey did catch on in the Copper Country as the area became the center for exciting ice hockey in the Midwest. When the Palace Ice Rink opened in 1899 it was the premier hockey venue with a large ice surface and seating for 1,000 spectators. The building was originally built as a smelter in the early 1890s by the Lake Superior Smelting Company on a site in Ripley immediately east of the Portage Lake Bridge and was converted to a natural ice rink for skating and hockey. The Palace became the home for several local hockey teams and leagues for three seasons before the Amphidrome opened in Houghton in December, 1902. The Palace was then used by the Hancock Central High School hockey team, but following a dispute it became a curling rink for several years before it was torn down.

CHAPTER 2: HOUGHTON AND THE COPPER COUNTRY ● 37

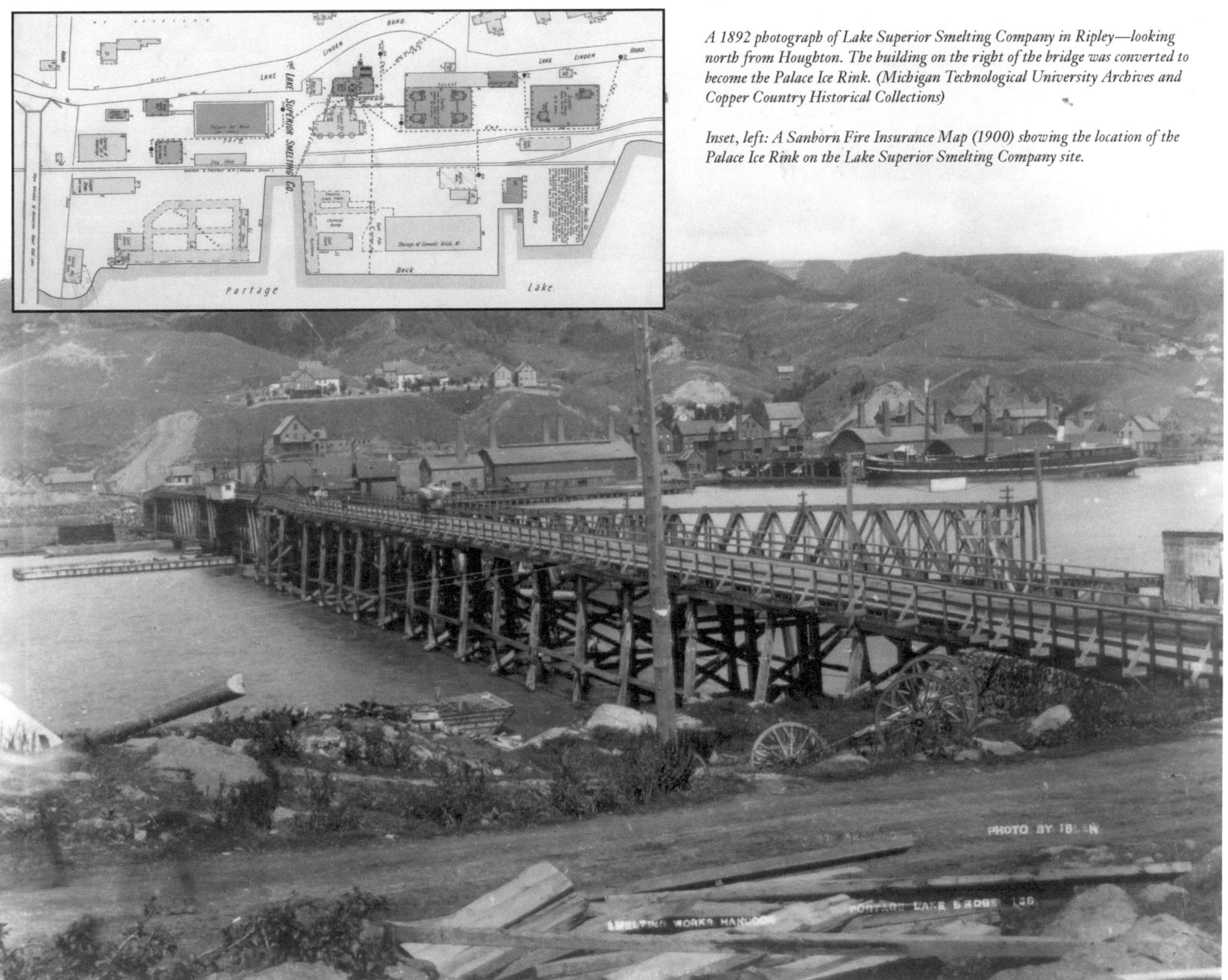

A 1892 photograph of Lake Superior Smelting Company in Ripley—looking north from Houghton. The building on the right of the bridge was converted to become the Palace Ice Rink. (Michigan Technological University Archives and Copper Country Historical Collections)

Inset, left: A Sanborn Fire Insurance Map (1900) showing the location of the Palace Ice Rink on the Lake Superior Smelting Company site.

38 • HOUGHTON: THE BIRTHPLACE OF PROFESSIONAL HOCKEY

A photograph of the Palace Ice Rink on the Portage waterfront, with Houghton in the background. (City of Houghton Ralph Raffaelli Collection)

CHAPTER 3
Gibson Comes to Houghton

SINCE HOCKEY WAS INTRODUCED IN THE COPPER Country by Ernest Yates and his Dollar Bay teammates new arenas opened, and several hockey teams and leagues soon formed. A note in the November 17, 1898 edition of the Houghton Daily Mining Gazette reflected the excitement for hockey.

"Hockey will soon be the fashion. If you want to keep up with the times, play hockey."

John L. "Jack" Gibson

One of the early hockey pioneers in the Copper Country was John Lindell MacDonald "Jack" Gibson. Gibson was born in Berlin (now Kitchener), Ontario on September 10, 1879 to James and Mary Gibson who were originally from Aberdeen, Scotland and settled on a farm in Waterloo County. Jack had six sisters and two brothers, attended schools in Berlin, and graduated from Pickering College (a private high school in Newmarket, Ontario) where he was captain of the hockey team. As a youth he excelled in school and several sports and won Western Ontario championships in rowing, skating, and swimming, and such were his soccer skills that he received an offer to play in the developmental system of the famous English Everton team but declined and decided to stay home and play hockey.

John Lindell MacDonald "Jack" Gibson, D.D.S. (Michigan Technological University Archives and Copper Country Historical Collections)

At seventeen he was a star member of the 1896–97 Berlin-Waterloo team in the Ontario Hockey Association's new intermediate league that defeated the Kingston Frontenacs to win the league championship. In the fall of 1897 Gibson entered the Detroit College of Medicine (now part of Wayne State University) to study dentistry and became a member of their hockey team. He also played on a Berlin senior team in the OHA league and planned to travel between Detroit and Berlin for games during the 1897–98 season. However, when the Berlin team defeated its crosstown rivals, Waterloo, in an early season game, team manager and Berlin Mayor Rumpel rushed out on the ice and presented each player with a ten dollar gold piece. The Ontario Hockey Association heard about this celebration and ruled that the players were professionals and expelled the team from further competition. Only amateurs "in good standing" were allowed to play in the OHA and players who received any remuneration were guilty until proven innocent. His season with Berlin ended in early January and although the OHA lifted its suspension at the end of the season, it left a lasting impression. Gibson played three seasons for the Detroit College of Medicine (DCM) hockey and football teams, and graduated in 1900. While he studied at DCM he continued to play soccer for the Berlin Rangers and a Berlin hockey club. The Berlin hockey club won every game in the 1899–1900 season and Gibson was recognized as one of best hockey players in Canada.

Detroit College of Medicine (DCM) Football Team 1899
(Wayne State University Library Archives)
Gibson is seated in the front row holding the ball. Gibson was team captain. Percy Willson and Earl Hay (to Gibson's right) were also members of the team. In the late 1800s the rules for college football were a mix of soccer and rugby and loosely based on those of the Football Association of London, England.

Detroit College of Medicine (DCM) Hockey Team 1887–98
(Michigan Technological University Archives and Copper Country Historical Collections)
Standing, left to right: *Frank Boles, Jack Gibson, Earl Hay.*
Seated, left to right: *F. Buggins, W. MacDonald, Percy Willson.*
Front Row, left to right: *Fred MacDonald, Wilson Randolph*

In the fall of 1900, Gibson moved to Houghton and established his dental practice in the Young Building on Shelden Avenue in downtown Houghton. He felt that this would be a perfect place to start his career as the area was in the midst of a copper mining boom and he had visited Houghton before when the DCM hockey team traveled to play an exhibition game at the Palace Ice Rink in Ripley. A couple of his DCM hockey teammates from Listowel, Ontario also chose to settle in the Copper Country. Dr. Earl Hay opened a dental office in Hancock and Dr. Percy Willson settled in Chassell to begin his practice as a medical doctor. A legendary story is that Merv Youngs, a reporter for the Houghton Daily Mining Gazette, apparently discovered a scrapbook of newspaper clippings in Gibson's office and wrote about this great sports figure in their midst.

Gibson was captain and coach of the Portage Lake team. Charles Webb was the team manager and responsible for the financial aspects and team operations. Webb was the Houghton agent for the Chicago and Northwestern Railroad and served as manager for Portage Lake clubs for many years. The Portage Lake team won the Upper Peninsula League Championship and local interest in hockey grew as fans packed the Palace Rink to see Gibson and the team play. The team brought considerable acclaim to the area by defeating a team from Sault Ste. Marie, Ontario, when the Sault team was advertised as the best in Ontario.

In January 1901, Gibson travelled to St. Louis with the Berlin Rangers soccer team to play three games against the top teams in St. Louis. A hockey game was also arranged between the Berlin Rangers and a St. Louis Association Football Hockey Club which featured some of St. Louis's best hockey players. Ice hockey had started in St. Louis a couple of years earlier when the St. Louis Ice Palace opened with artificial ice and a local league was organized with teams of transplanted Canadians and lawyers and bankers who had played on Ivy League university clubs. Gibson put on an amazing demonstration of hockey skills and the Berlin team of soccer players defeated the St. Louis team. The St. Louis team was not discouraged and regrouped by adding a few of the best players from other St. Louis teams to become the St. Louis World Fair 1904's team and they traveled to Houghton a couple of years later to play Portage Lake.

Berlin Hockey Club, 1899–1900—*Champions of Western Ontario Hockey Association*
(City of Kitchener)
Standing, left to right: *P. Thompson (spare), Oliver Seibert (forward), Jack Gibson (point), W.E. Gowling (secretary-treasurer), Joe Stephens (forward), A. Shantz (trainer)*
Seated, left to right: *J. Roos (forward), G.N. Elliot (manager), Carlo Boehmer (cover point and captain), L. Krueger (goal), R. Cossey (spare)*

The 1900–01 Portage Lake YMCA Hockey Team

Gibson immersed himself in the Houghton community, joined several fraternal lodges, and met community leaders through social events. He soon became known as "Doc" Gibson and in his first winter he joined the Portage Lake YMCA hockey team. The team included several local players, as well as Dr. Hay, Dr. Willson, and Dr. R.B. Harkness. Dr. Harkness, a medical doctor, was born in Pennsylvania and played hockey in Pittsburgh as a student at Western University of Pennsylvania (now the University of Pittsburgh). He moved to Houghton in the fall of 1900 and located his office in the Young Building in downtown Houghton—the same building as Gibson. Harkness was also in charge of the local weather bureau.

Portage Lake YMCA Hockey Team, 1900–01
(City of Houghton, Ralph Raffaelli Collection)
Standing, left to right: *Bert Potter, Ellsworth, R.B. Harkness, Black, Earl Hay*

Seated, left to right: *Wally Washburn, Jack Gibson, Charles Webb, Percy Willson, Peter Delaney*
Front Row, left to right: *Thompson, Andy Haller*

The 1901–02 Portage Lake Hockey Team

As the Portage Lake team prepared for the 1901–02 season, Houghton businessman James R. Dee joined the executive board, and Gibson and Webb started to recruit a few players from outside the Copper Country. Gibson brought in Herman "Dutch" Meinke with whom he had played in Berlin and recruited Joseph "Chief" Jones, one of the best goalies in Ontario, from Renfrew, Ontario; Bobby Rowe from Barrie, Ontario; and Edward "Ted" Howell from Guelph, Ontario. Games were scheduled with teams from Minneapolis, St. Paul, Chicago, Pittsburgh, and Sault Ste. Marie, Ontario and new brown sweaters with PL letters on the front were purchased from A.G. Spalding and Company. Spalding was the major hockey and sporting goods equipment manufacturer in the United States during this era, and were also known for publishing a library of "How to Play" sports books. The author of Spalding's How to Play Hockey was Art Farrell, a former teammate of Gibson's on the 1898 Berlin hockey team. Dr. Harkness was the referee for all of the team's home games at the Palace Rink.

The team started the season with a victory against Ernest Yates' Dollar Bay team and they played ten games that season, losing only once to the Pittsburgh Athletic Club in the last game of the season. In February, Portage Lake played an all-star team of the best players from Sault Ste. Marie, Ontario (referred to as "Canadian Soo"), but prior to the game the Sault team felt that Portage Lake's Ted Howell was seen as a professional player by the Ontario Hockey Association (OHA) so they did not want him to play. At the time, Canadian teams were concerned that if they played a team with professional players, the OHA would rule that they had professional players and would be ruled ineligible for any provincial competitions. Howell did not play but Portage Lake still defeated the Sault team.

Portage Lake was declared Upper Peninsula Champion and Champions of the West after they defeated the Kenwood Country Club team from Chicago. The team then played the Pittsburgh Athletic Club in March 1902 for what was described as the Championship of the United States. Pittsburgh was the Eastern Champion. It was to be a two game, total goals series in the Palace. The team split the games and the total goals were equal so a 1902 United States Champion was not declared.

Results from the Portage Lake 1901–02 Season

January 7, 1902	Portage Lake 6	Dollar Bay 3	Palace
January 24	Portage Lake 7	Minneapolis 4	Minneapolis
January 25	Portage Lake 2	St. Paul 0	St. Paul
February 1	Portage Lake 5	Canadian Soo 4	Palace
February 14	Portage Lake 11	St. Paul 1	Palace
February 15	Portage Lake 12	St. Paul 1	Palace
February 21	Portage Lake 5	Chicago 0 (Kenwood Country Club)	Palace
February 22	Portage Lake 8	Chicago 0 (Kenwood Country Club)	Palace
March 10	Portage Lake 5	Pittsburgh Athletic Club 4	Palace
March 11	Portage Lake 2	Pittsburgh Athletic Club 3	Palace

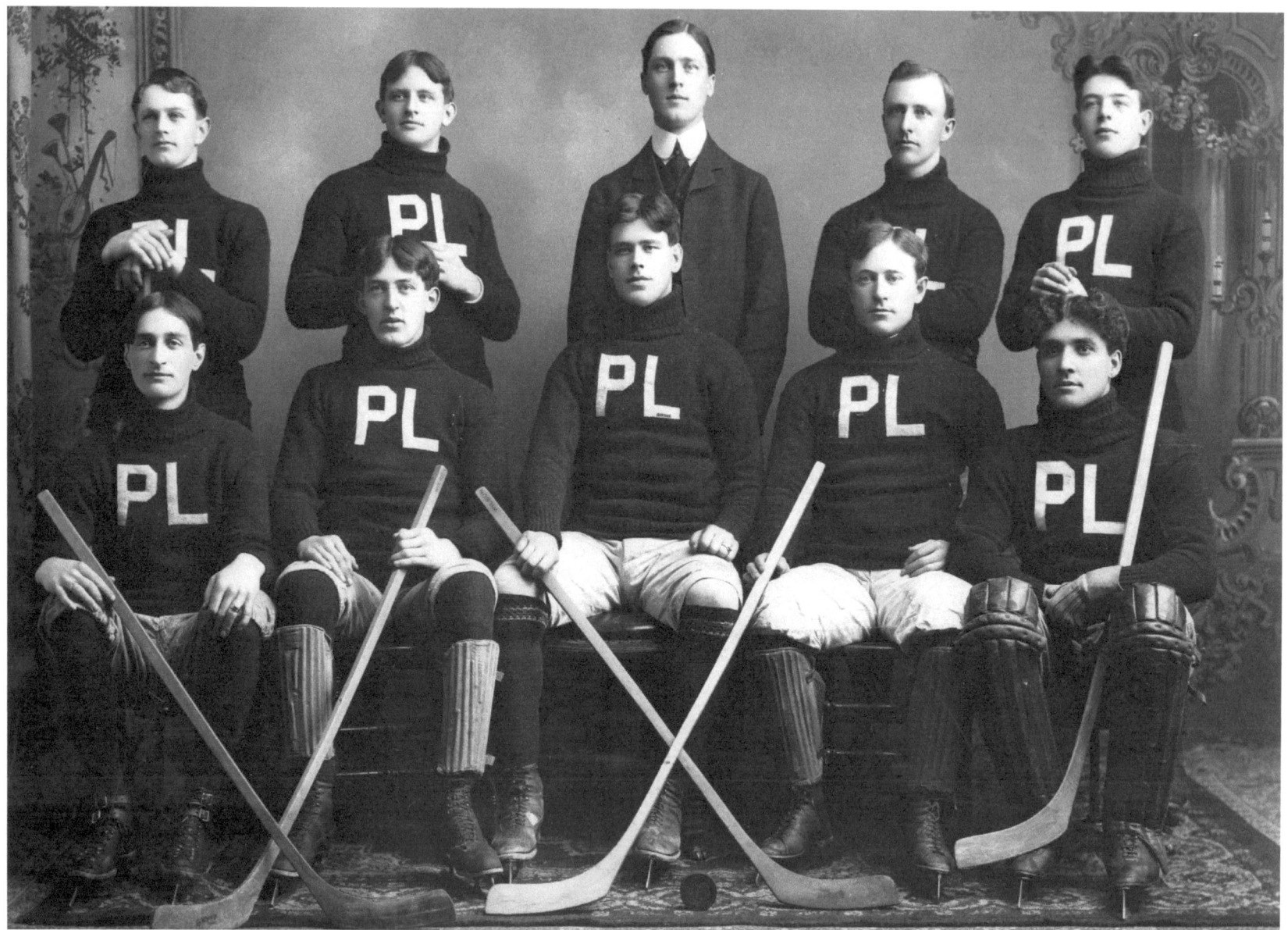

Portage Lake Hockey Team, 1901–02—*Champions of the West* (Michigan Technological University Archives and Copper Country Historical Collections) Standing, left to right: *Andy Haller (rover), Earl Hay (spare), Charles Webb (manager), Percy Willson (center), Bobby Rowe (forward)*

Front Row, left to right: *Wally Washburn (spare), Herman "Dutch" Meinke (forward), Jack Gibson (cover point and captain), Edward Howell (point), Joseph Henry "Chief" Jones (goal)*

The Championship Hockey Games Of the West

To be played at the Palace Ice Rink, Friday, Feb. 21 and Saturday afternoon, Feb. 22, between

Kenwood Country Club (Chicago.)

AND

Portage Lake Hockey Club

This game will undoubtedly be the finest game ever played in the west. The Kenwood club has not been beaten, and have a score of 132 goals to their credit. The Portage Lake team has yet to see defeat.

It Will Be a Battle Royal.

Special trains from all over the county and excellent street car accommodations.

Newspaper Advertisement for Games between Kenwood Country Club (Chicago) and Portage Lake at the Palace Ice Rink (1902) for the Championship of the West (City of Houghton Ralph Raffaelli Collection)

The Amphidrome

The capacity of the Palace Ice Rink was 1,000 spectators and many had to be turned away for the best games. Gibson and Dee soon realized that if hockey were to grow in the area, a new facility would be needed to accommodate the spectators that wanted to see the Portage Lake team play. In the summer of 1902, local entrepreneurs in the Houghton area began planning for a new indoor arena. Dee organized the Houghton Warehouse Company to build a facility that could be used as a storage warehouse and serve as a skating and hockey arena during the winter months. The company purchased property on the Houghton waterfront from the Ruppe family. They felt that the location was ideal for the loading and unloading ships and it was adjacent to the Duluth, South Shore and Atlantic Railroad main line. It was a few blocks from the Copper Range Railroad depot, close to the Duluth, South Shore and Atlantic (Mineral Range) Railroad passenger depot, and one block from the Houghton streetcar line. The Chicago construction firm of Prendergast and Clarkson was awarded the contract in mid-November and to finish construction in time for the winter season, the project employed the largest number

Amphidrome under construction on the Portage Lake waterfront in Houghton (City of Houghton, Ralph Raffaelli Collection)

The Houghton Amphidrome (City of Houghton Ralph Raffaelli Collection)

of carpenters to ever work on a building in the Houghton area at that time. The natural ice surface was 80 feet by 185 feet and the arena had seating for 2,500 hockey fans and room for an additional 600 standees. The cost of the building was $16,000 and would be available for skating and hockey from early December until late March. A contest to name the facility was held and Mrs. E. C. Taylor of East Houghton won a $5 gold coin and $2 worth of skating tickets for the name "Amphidrome." Other names that were suggested included the Colliseum, Metropolitan, Arena Roosevelt, Copper Dome, Pride of the North, Houghton Arena, and the Wooden Elephant. Local residents would usually refer to the arena as "The Drome."

Interior of the Amphidrome (Michigan Technological University Archives and Copper Country Historical Collections).

The 1902–03 Portage Lake Hockey Team

While the arena was being built, Gibson and Webb were busy recruiting better players from Canada for the upcoming season. They brought in Joe Stephens, one of Gibson's teammates from Berlin, and Fred Lake and Ernie Westcott, who had played for Pittsburgh in the Western Pennsylvania Hockey League. The team adopted green and white sweaters and the winged PL logo from Gibson's Berlin team.

The Amphidrome opened soon after Christmas in 1902 and the first hockey game was played on Monday, December 29, 1902 between Portage Lake and the University of Toronto Varsity team. The local newspaper reported that over 5,000 attended the first game and it was the largest gathering of people under one roof in the Upper Peninsula at that time. Portage Lake beat the team from Toronto 13-2 and the top scorer was center Herbert "Dutch" Meinke as he scored 8 goals. Dr. Percy Willson was the referee and the Calumet and Hecla Band played before, during, and after the game.

The 1902–03 Portage Lake hockey team was a good team that went undefeated for the season and outscored their opponents 146-36. The schedule evolved as Webb worked to arrange games during the season. All of their games, except for the final two games of the season, were played at the Amphidrome as it was seen as the premier arena in the country and everyone wanted to play in this new facility. Portage Lake played 16 games against teams from Detroit, Duluth, St. Louis, St. Paul, and Pittsburgh and they defeated the Pittsburgh Bankers for the United States Championship. Joe Stephens and Dutch Meinke were the season's top scorers for Portage Lake with 36 goals and 34 goals, respectively.

Off the ice, Gibson was a star promoter of hockey. Local newspapers sought comments and he would wax poetically in predicting a promising future for hockey as the best winter sport in America. Following the successful season, Gibson, Webb, and Dee immediately started to think about the next season.

James R. Dee

James Rogers "Jimmy" Dee was born at Cliff Mine, Michigan on November 11, 1856; his father was a miner and his family immigrated to the Keweenaw from Ireland in 1850. He had four brothers—John, Thomas, William, and Martin. As a teenager James moved to Houghton and became a messenger boy for the Western Union Company and worked as a bell boy in the Continental Hotel. In just a few months he mastered the telegraph and was given an operator's position in Eagle Harbor, but six months later he was transferred back to Houghton and became the manager of Western Union operations in the Copper Country. A few years later while on vacation in Philadelphia he discovered a new gadget called the telephone and when he returned to Houghton he devoted his efforts in introducing a telephone system to the area under the Michigan Bell Telephone. His next project was organizing the Peninsula Electric Light and Power Company and a few years later he formed the Houghton County Street Railway Company. Dee became a real estate developer and built several buildings in downtown including the Shelden-Dee Building, the Gazette building, the Dee Hotel, the Board of Trade building (now the Library restaurant), and led the expansion of the Douglass House hotel, and built Houghton's first bowling alleys and the first motion picture theatre.

Dee served on the local council and was founding member of the Portage Lake Golf Club, Onigaming Yacht Club, and the Copper Country Agricultural Association. Dee enjoyed sports and in 1902 he organized the Houghton Warehouse Company to build the Amphidrome, and was involved in organizing the first professional baseball league in the Copper Country and the first professional hockey league. Dee contributed in so many ways as a community leader in business and civic activities and died on December 24, 1946 at the age of 90.

Shelden-Dee Building in Downtown Houghton (Michigan Technological University Archives and Copper Country Historical Collections)
The Shelden-Dee Building opened in 1900 at the corner of Isle Royale and Shelden. It was built by Dee and Mary Shelden, wife of successful businessman George Shelden, as a commercial building in downtown Houghton. George Shelden originally purchased the property for the building but died before the project was completed. The building included several stores, offices, and the Board of Trade Café.

Douglass House in Downtown Houghton
(Michigan Technological University Archives and Copper Country Historical Collections)
The original Douglass House was built in 1860 on the corner of Isle Royale and Montezuma Streets, with a garden stretching to Shelden Street. In 1899 a group of Houghton investors, including Dee, purchased the hotel and added a new addition fronting on Shelden. The Douglass House was one of the finest hotels in the Upper Peninsula.

James Rogers "Jimmy" Dee (City of Houghton Ralph Raffaelli Collection)

Portage Lake Hockey Team, 1902–03—Champions of the United States
(Michigan Technological University Archives and Copper Country Historical Collections)
Standing, left to right: Andy Haller (spare), Joe Stephens (rover), Charley Webb (manager), L.J. Ames (trainer), Jack Baker (point).

Seated, left to right: Jack Gibson (cover point and captain), Bobby Rowe (forward), Joseph Henry "Chief" Jones (goal), Ernie Westcott (forward), Herman "Dutch" Meinke (forward), Paddy (mascot)

HOCKEY IS THE FASTEST GAME

Captain Gibson of the Portage Lakes Tells of the Attractions of the Great Ice Game and its Superiority.

Hockey is the chief subject of conversation with Portage lake people these days and everyone is looking forward eagerly to the night when the local team of which so much is rightly expected can try its mettle against the crack seven from the Toronto Varsity. That hockey is a game which is growing in popularity by leaps and bounds no one can doubt. It seems destined to be the great winter sport of the northern tier of states as it is already of the provinces of Canada. The game has no more enthusiastic follower very naturally than Captain Gibson of the Portage lake team, and because of his long experience and his great ability as a player the following ideas from him about the game will be of great interest to readers of The Mining Gazette.

"The attractions and popularity of hockey as a cold weather game are rapidly increasing. It has much to commend it to public favor, with its requirements of swiftness, grace, dash and adroitness. It is not a sport for the weak or the stupid. Every faculty is kept alert and the demands on the brain, as well as on the nerves and sinews, are constant. Strategy and daring, ingenuity and nimbleness are requisites for success. It is even more exciting for the teams and the spectators than polo in the summer and the pace is far quicker. As matters look now, hockey has a highly promising future among the best winter sports in America.

The Calumet and Hecla Band played at the first game at the Amphidrome, December 29, 1902. Bands were common at hockey and other sporting events during that era. The Quincy Band and Quincy Excelsior Band were other bands that performed at local hockey games. (Michigan Technological University Archives and Copper Country Historical Collections)

Houghton Daily Mining Gazette, December 17, 1902 (Hockey is the Fastest Game)

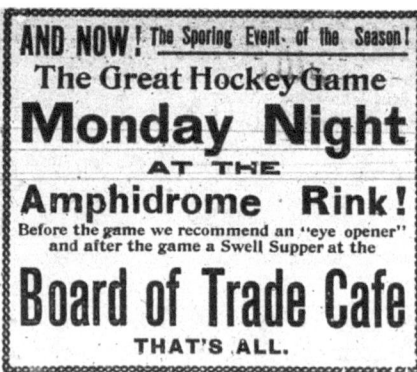

Ad for the Board of Trade Café for the opening game at the Amphidrome

UNIVERSITY TEAM TAKEN INTO CAMP

Portage Lakes Defeat Visitors From Toronto by Score of 13 to 2.

GAME, HARD FOUGHT BATTLE

Meinke, Westcott and Gibson Stars of Local Seven and Woods and Evans for the 'Varsity.

If there has been any doubt as to whether or not Portage Lake was to have a hockey team of championship class this year, that doubt was dispelled last night when Captain Gibson and his men in the first game of the year defeated the strong seven from Toronto 'Varsity in brilliant style by the score of 13 to 2. The Portage Lakes played a whirlwind game from start to finish and at no time after the first ten minutes of the game had elapsed was there any doubt as to the final outcome. In fact till the middle of the second half it looked as though the 'Varsity boys would be shut out entirely. The game was not, however, a walkaway, as the score might seem to indicate. None of the Portage Lake goals were won on flukes and all of them came only after the hardest kind of fighting and the most brilliant play.

The 'Varsity boys never thought of letting up for a moment and were contesting as hard after defeat was certain as they did in the first few moments after the face off. The Toronto boys are not to be held lightly because of their decisive defeat. They are a good seven, and also, they are the seven of the Toronto 'Varsity. A report was circulated here last night that the seven which played here was not the real 'Varsity seven. That report was false. The team which lined up against Portage Lake last night was the strongest the Toronto boys could get together. The college boys were just outclassed. That tells by the score story of the game.

Toronto expected to win. They had beaten the strong team of the Canadian Soo and figuring on that they concluded they had a little more than an even chance to trail the green and white. But the Toronto collegians will have to take a new course in comparative calculation.

Of the Portage Lake players Meinke and Stevens were the stars on defense. Rowe played a good game, but was not so fortunate in getting as many good shots for goal as his team mates. Jones played his usual reliable game at goal, spoiling some beautiful shots by Wood and others of the 'Varsity team. Westcott was everywhere and came out of every mix up ahead. As a usual thing he was too much for two of the opposing players. Baker at point did some good work at critical moments, but sometimes seemed slow in getting ahead. Captain Gibson played in old time form. He kept his head all the time and made the 'Varsity boys look like three cents when it came to dodging. Time and again he carried the puck nearly the length of the rink past the entire 'Varsity line.

The Portage Lake team work was excellent considering this was the first game of the year. For the 'Varsity Wood was easily the star of the game. His bright blue jersey flashed everywhere and he was constantly causing the Portage Lake defense all kinds of trouble. He is nearly as fast as Captain Gibson and shoots accurately. Captain Evans played a strong game at point. Lash is an excellent goalie. He foiled a dozen chances for goals and nothing got past him without a hard fight.

The game was played before an assembly of nearly 5,000 people. Special trains were run from all parts of the county and many people from faraway points attended. The line-up of the teams were as follows:

Portage Lake		'Varsity
Jones	G.	Lash
Baker	P.	Evans (Capt.)
Gibson (Capt.)	C. P.	Brown
Westcott	R. W.	Caulfield
Rowe	L. W.	Stone
Meinke	C.	Wood
Stevens	R.	Housser

Newspaper story on the first game at the Amphidrome, Houghton Daily Mining Gazette, December 30, 1902.

Results from the Portage Lake 1902–03 Season

December 27, 1902	Portage Lake 13	University of Toronto 2	Amphidrome
January 23, 1903	Portage Lake 20	St. Paul 2	Amphidrome
January 24	Portage Lake 8	St. Paul 6	Amphidrome
January 30	Portage Lake 13	St. Louis 0	Amphidrome
January 31	Portage Lake 10	St. Louis 1	Amphidrome
February 4	Portage Lake 11	Detroit 2	Amphidrome
February 5	Portage Lake 12	Detroit 3	Amphidrome
February 9	Portage Lake 10	Pittsburgh Victorias 1	Amphidrome
February 10	Portage Lake 7	Pittsburgh Victorias 6	Amphidrome
February 12	Portage Lake 13	Duluth 0	Amphidrome
February 23	Portage Lake 11	Pittsburgh Athletic Club 1	Amphidrome
February 24	Portage Lake 3	Pittsburgh Athletic Club 1	Amphidrome
March 2	Portage Lake 2	Pittsburgh Bankers 2	Amphidrome
March 3	Portage Lake 1	Pittsburgh Bankers 0	Amphidrome
March 20	Portage Lake 11	Pittsburgh Bankers 8	Duquesne Arena
March 21	Portage Lake 2	Pittsburgh Bankers 1	Duquesne Arena

A Hockey Fan in this Era

Early hockey games of the 1880s were social events and fans came as they might to a theatre for a play to mingle with friends and watch the production. Buffet tables were often set at half time so that players and fans could enjoy a feast before the players returned to action of the second half. The casual atmosphere on the ice and in the stands of these early games began to change when more people started to attend the games. As money became more prevalent, the games began to get more intense as team and city rivalries began to emerge.

As hockey grew, spectators began to overflow the small seating capacities of the game's earliest indoor rinks and rink owners were quick to realize that more money could be made from hockey than pleasure skating and they began to build new, larger arenas specifically for hockey. Some of the early rinks could be mistaken for barns or warehouses (built for skating and curling) and many would have posts in the middle of the ice surface and few seats for spectators. New arenas opened with better sight lines and seating. The temperature inside the rink was usually the same as the temperature outside so spectators came dressed in large coats, boots, and gloves, and some used baked potatoes as hand warmers or rested their boots on heated bricks that they prepared at home before the game. Spectators would drink hot coffee or alcohol refreshments to take off the chill. Smoking was common and a heavy cloud formed in the building.

The games lasted sixty minutes with a ten minute intermission, so rink owners and hockey promoters would use special promotions and events to attract spectators. Skating races, community bands and orchestras were a common feature of these early games. Spectators or rooters often came with horns, megaphones, and other noise making devices, and would organize cheers and devise other ways of supporting their teams. Streetcar service was common in many communities and special hockey trains with special low, round trip fares, would take local fans to out-of-town games to support their team. On longer trips, these trains would often have a party atmosphere. For fans who did not travel to out-of-town games, they would often gather at local hotels to hear telegraph reports of away games.

In many arenas, men would be the largest part of the audience and needless to say there would often be disagreements in the stands with everything from boots to chairs and various other items thrown onto the ice. Profane language, fighting, gambling and betting occurred and the charged atmosphere within a confined location was truly exciting.

Adapted from "Being a Hockey Fan in 1900," Howard Mickoski, in *Total Hockey*, Second Edition, Total Sports Publishing: Toronto, Ontario, 2000.

CHAPTER 4
Professional Hockey Begins in Houghton

THE 1902–03 PORTAGE LAKE TEAM WENT UNDEFEATED for the season and won the United States Championship, but Gibson felt that the team could be even better, so soon after the season ended Gibson and Webb started to recruit players for the next season and James Dee became President of the Portage Lake team.

The 1903–04 Portage Lake Hockey Team

In the fall of 1903, Gibson and Dee made a momentous decision when they resolved to openly pay players to come to Houghton to play hockey. They realized that to convince top Canadian players to give up day jobs to play hockey for a few months and risk their amateur status in Canada, substantial salaries were essential. Individual player contracts were negotiated and salaries that paid $15 to $40 per week were enough to convince players to take the risk. The best players could attract a salary of $75 per week. Salaries would come from dividing gate receipts.

Gibson and Webb recruited several players from the Pittsburgh teams including Riley Hern, Bert Morrison, Billy "Cooney" Shields, and Bruce and Hod Stuart for the Portage Lake team. A group from Sault Ste. Marie, Michigan also decided to pay players and several members of 1902–03 Portage Lake team signed to join the Michigan Soo team. Former Portage Lake players included Chief Jones, Herman Meinke, Joe Stephens, Fred Lake, Jack Baker, and Andy Haller. The Michigan Soo team also recruited Billy Hamilton and Frank Switzer from Pittsburgh.

The Portage Lake line up for the season included:

Doc Gibson (hometown: Berlin, Ontario; 1902–03 team: Portage Lake)—cover point and captain

Riley Hern (hometown: St. Mary's, Ontario; 1902–03 team: Pittsburgh Keystones)—goal

Bert Morrison (hometown: Toronto, Ontario; 1902–03 team: New York Athletic Club, 1901–02 team: Pittsburgh Keystones)—rover

"Cooney" Shields (hometown: Guelph, Ontario; 1902–03 teams: Pittsburgh Athletic Club and Pittsburgh Bankers)—right wing

Bruce Stuart (hometown: Ottawa, Ontario; 1902–03 team: Pittsburgh Victorias)—center

Hod Stuart (hometown: Ottawa, Ontario; 1902–03 team: Pittsburgh Bankers)—point

Ernie Westcott (hometown: Beaverton, Ontario; 1902–03 team: Portage Lake)—left wing

Fred Westcott and Joe Linder were spares on the team and played only a few games during the season when members of the team were injured or not available for a game. Joe Linder was a sophomore at Hancock Central High School and a star athlete in hockey, football, and baseball when Gibson recruited him for a few games with the Portage Lake team. Although Linder only dressed for three games he was in the team photograph.

The expectations for a successful season were very high in the community as the local newspapers wrote that the recruited players were among the best from Canada. Because the team was not in a league, exhibition games were arranged and the schedule evolved during the season. The season started with one-sided victories over teams from St. Paul and St. Louis in December so Gibson and Webb sought better competition and although they wanted to arrange games with the best teams from Canada, Ontario teams were reluctant to schedule games as they would be banned by the Ontario Hockey Association.

Games were scheduled with the Michigan Soo team and the four Pittsburgh teams from the Western Pennsylvania Hockey League (WPHL) and in spite of the potential ban by the OHA, Webb was able to schedule two games against a team from Sault Ste. Marie, Ontario. A new arena had been built in Soo Canada with borrowed money and there was no serious competition in the area, so the newly formed Algonquin Hockey Club turned to Michigan Soo and Portage Lake for games. The Canadian Soo team played both Portage Lake and Michigan Soo but managed only a 1-5-1 record against the two teams and was suspended by the OHA.

Portage Lake had an outstanding team and defeated the Pittsburgh Victorias in a three-game series at the Duquesne Gardens in Pittsburgh for the United States Championship. As the season ended and the team returned to Houghton where there was some talk of submitting a challenge for the Stanley Cup, but soon after their arrival Webb received

PORTAGE LAKE'S ARE CHAMPIONS

Victorias Were Shut Out in the Decisive Game of Series. Score 7 to 0

CONTEST FAST AND CLEAN

Shields Executed the Most Brilliant Play by Making a Goal Without Any Assistance.

(Special to The Mining Gazette.)
Pittsburg, Pa., March 15. — The hockey championship goes to Houghton, the crack Portage Lake team from northern Michigan skating rings around the Victorias last night at Duquesne Garden in the decisive games of the series, winning by the one-sided score of 7 to 0. The Victorias were never in the hunt at any stage and the outcome was a forgone conclusion at the end of the first half, when the tally stood 2 to 0 in favor of the visitors.

Played in Brilliant Form.

Portage Lake played up to their brilliant form of last Saturday night, while the local champions appeared slow...

Victorias.		Portage Lake.
Mackay	goal	Hern
Duval	point	Gibson
...	c point	H. Stuart
A. Sixsmith	center	B. Stuart
E. Roberts	rover	Morrison
J. Roberts	l. wing	Shields
G. Sixsmith	r. wing	Westcott

Goals—B. Stuart 2, Morrison 3, Shields and Westcott.
Referee—Schooley. Goal judges—T. Ross and Melville of P. A. C. Time, two 20 minute halves.

Newspaper report on final game of Pittsburg vs. Portage Game Series—Portage Lake are U.S. Champions, Houghton Daily Mining Gazette, *March 16, 1904.*

PORTAGE LAKE'S WELCOMED HOME

Victorious Hockey Players Welcomed by a Great Demonstration Yesterday When They Returned from Pittsburg.

Bands and banners and bunting were in evidence early yesterday morning and all day for that matter and Houghton had on its holiday attire to welcome home the victorious Portage Lake hockey club after its trip of conquest to Pittsburg.

The businessmen were out early to decorate the fronts of their stores and offices with the green and white, the colors which the local seven had carried to victory and the championship of the United States in the greatest of winter sports. The Quincy band started the excitement with a selection in front of the Douglass house and then led the crowd to the Mineral Range depot to welcome the boys home.

The coming of the train was noted far down the lake by the blowing of the big steam whistles on mills and foundries and as the train approached those nearer Houghton took up the blast till the air was filled with a crash of sound, a mighty welcome to the Portage Lakes.

The station was crowded with people, every available inch of space on every available point of view was taken up with a yelling mob of people and when the train pulled up the Portage Lakes were greeted with a mighty cheer.

The boys all returned in perfect condition and good spirits. They showed no ill effects from the rough usage accorded them in Pittsburg. They were immediately taken in hand by the Amphidrome management and carried to the Douglass House, their triumphal progress being headed by the Quincy band. At the Douglass House they were the guests of John C. Mann for dinner.

Welcome home to Portage Lake championship team, Houghton Daily Mining Gazette, *March 19, 1904.*

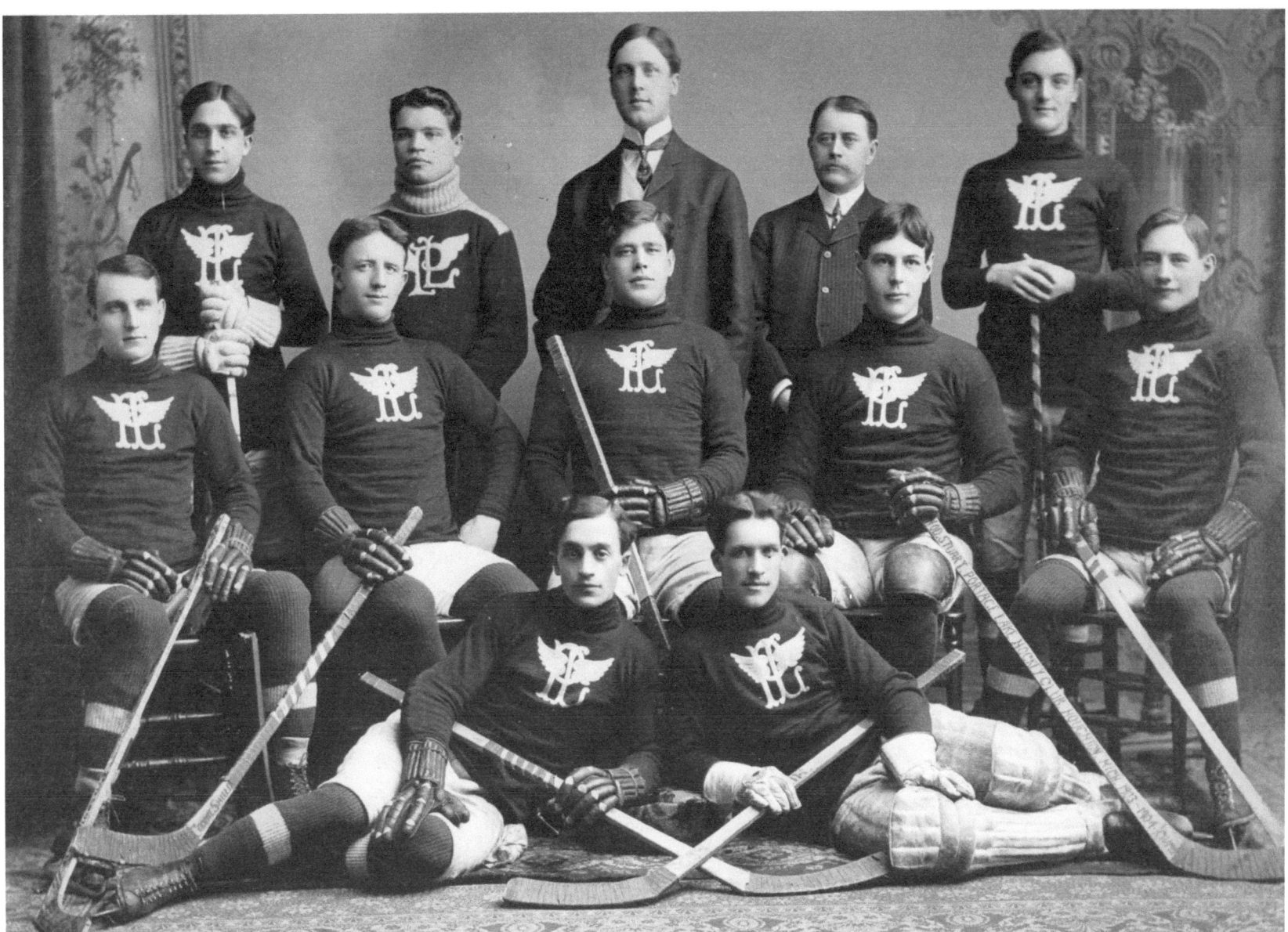

Portage Lake Hockey Team, 1903–04—U.S. Champion and World Champion
(Michigan Technological University Archives and Copper Country Historical Collections)

Standing left to right: *Fred Westcott (spare), James Duggan (trainer), Charles Webb (manager), James Dee (president), Joe Linder (spare)*. Seated left to right: *Bert Morrison (rover), "Cooney" Shields (forward), "Doc" Gibson (point and captain), Hod Stuart (cover point), Bruce Stuart (forward)*. In foreground: *Ernie Westcott (forward), Riley Hern (goal)*

Cartoon to celebrate the Portage Lake team arrival home after winning 1904 U.S. Championship. (Jim and John Leech Collection)

a challenge from the Montreal Wanderers of the Federal Amateur Hockey League for a two-game series to be played in Houghton.

In early March, the Montreal Wanderers challenged the current Stanley Cup holder, the Ottawa Hockey Club, to a two-game series with the first game to be played in Montreal and the second game in Ottawa. The first game was held in Montreal on March 2, 1904 and the teams played to a 5-5 tie at the end of regulation time. However the Wanderers refused to play overtime with the current referee.

The Cup trustees ordered the series to restart with both games to be played in Ottawa. The Wanderers refused to continue the series unless the tie was replayed in Montreal. The Wanderers were disqualified and forfeited the series, but as the champions of the Federal Amateur Hockey League they felt that they were the best team in Canada.

The Ottawa Hockey Club had won the Stanley Cup following the 1903 season when they defeated the Montreal Victorias, and each Ottawa player received a silver nugget from team director and mining investor Bob Shillington. He gave them nuggets instead of money since the players were still technically amateurs and to give them money would have meant disqualification and suspensions by the OHA. After receiving the nuggets one of the players is to have said, "We should call ourselves the Silver Seven," and the name caught on. The Ottawa Silver Seven were challenged several times in the following years, including the famous series with the Dawson City Nuggets in January 1905. The Montreal Wanderers and Ottawa would again meet for the Stanley Cup in 1906 and the Wanderers were successful in taking the Cup from Ottawa.

Portage Lake accepted the challenge and two games were scheduled for March 21 and 22, 1904 in the Amphidrome. The series was billed as the World Championship between the Montreal Wanderers, Champions of Canada, and Portage Lake, Champions of the United States. Portage Lake defeated the Wanderers in the first game 8-4, and according to local newspaper reports, "the game was the fastest hockey ever exhibited in the Copper Country and naturally the greatest game ever played in the United States." On the following night, Portage Lake defeated the Wanderers 9-2, and the newspaper stated that, "the game had all the features which go to make hockey the most exciting sport in the world."

One of the Portage Lake players was quoted, "We claim to be champions of the world and ready to play any team which disputes our claim to the title and willing to produce all kinds of money to back it."

Newspaper advertisement for World's Championship series between Montreal Wanderers and Portage Lake, 1904

Montreal Wanderers Team, 1904
Standing left to right: *Cecil Blachford, Billy Strachan, Billy Bellingham, Bert Strachan*
Seated left to right: *Ken Mallen, Dickie Boon, Billy Nicholson*
In foreground: *Jack Marshall, Jimmy Gardner*

Ken Mallen and Billy Nicholson would later play three seasons for the Calumet team in the International Hockey League (IHL) and Jimmy Gardner played two seasons for Calumet and one season for Pittsburgh in the IHL.

Results from the 1903–04 Season

December 17, 1903	Portage Lake 20	St. Paul Victorias 0	Amphidrome
December 19	Portage Lake 15	St. Paul Victorias 1	Amphidrome
December 25	Portage Lake 21	St. Louis World's Fair Club 0	Amphidrome
December 26*	Portage Lake 24	St. Louis World's Fair Club 0	Amphidrome
January 1, 1904	Portage Lake 16	Canadian Soo 1	Amphidrome
January 2	Portage Lake 7	Canadian Soo 0	Amphidrome
January 13	Portage Lake 6	Michigan Soo 1	Amphidrome
January 14	Portage Lake 12	Michigan Soo 1	Amphidrome
January 18	Portage Lake 9	Pittsburgh Keystones 4	Amphidrome
January 19	Portage Lake 12	Pittsburgh Keystones 1	Amphidrome
January 23	Portage Lake 6	Michigan Soo 7	Soo MI Curling Rink
January 25	Portage Lake 4	Michigan Soo 1	Soo MI Curling Rink
January 28	Portage Lake 11	Pittsburgh Athletic Club 1	Amphidrome
January 29	Portage Lake 6	Pittsburgh Athletic Club 3	Amphidrome
February 4	Portage Lake 14	Pittsburgh Bankers 7	Amphidrome
February 5	Portage Lake 14	Pittsburgh Bankers 5	Amphidrome
February 16	Portage Lake 9	Michigan Soo 1	Amphidrome
February 17	Portage Lake 11	Michigan Soo 1	Amphidrome
February 20	Portage Lake 6	Michigan Soo 1	Soo MI Curling Rink
February 21	Portage Lake 5	Michigan Soo 1	Soo MI Curling Rink
March 11	Portage Lake 2	Pittsburgh Victorias 5	Duquesne Gardens
March 12	Portage Lake 5	Pittsburgh Victorias 1	Duquesne Gardens
March 15	Portage Lake 7	Pittsburgh Victorias 0	Duquesne Gardens
March 21	Portage Lake 8	Montreal Wanderers 4	Amphidrome
March 22	Portage Lake 9	Montreal Wanderers 2	Amphidrome

*A tragic story following the December series with the St. Louis World's Fair team involved their captain and star player Harry Kiely. Kiely was also a professor at St. Louis University and after the series he stopped in Chicago to visit his sister while the rest of the team returned to St. Louis. On the afternoon of December 30, Kiely and his sister went to a matinee performance of the musical Mr. Blue Beard at the recently opened Iroquois Theater. A fire broke out in the theater and over 600 people died, including Kiely and his sister. It is still the deadliest single-building fire in U.S. history.

Portage Lake ended the season with a record of 23 wins and 2 losses, and they outscored their opponents 259 to 49. The team was undefeated in 18 home games and their two losses occurred away from the Amphidrome—one in Sault Michigan and one in Pittsburgh. Dr. Percy Willson was referee for 12 of the home games at the Amphidrome.

Bert Morrison proved his value to Portage Lake as he scored 94 goals and Bruce Stuart wasn't far behind as he scored 75 goals. Riley Hern was the goalie for all 25 games and recorded five shutouts with a goals against average of 1.96 goals per game.

Player	Games Played	Goals
Bert Morrison	25	94
Bruce Stuart	25	75
"Cooney" Shields	25	37
Hod Stuart	25	17
Ernie Westcott	22	24
"Doc" Gibson	23	10
Fred Westcott	3	2
Joe Linder	3	0
Goal: Riley Hern	25	

In Michigan Soo, Frank Switzer scored 45 goals in 24 games while former Portage Lake players Herman Meinke scored 37 goals and Fred Lake scored 28 goals.

Following their victory for the World's Championship, jewelry was given to the players and several songs and marches were composed on their behalf. One of the marches is the "March Amphidrome" composed by Conrad Sagemiller, a local musical artist who played in several local bands. He was born in Germany but had immigrated to the Copper Country as a young boy and dedicated the March to the Portage Lake team out of respect for the publicity that they bought to the Copper Country. It cost Sagemiller $90 to get the Portage Lake players to sit for the photograph that appears on the cover of the sheet music. Later in the year, Sagemiller composed music to remember those who died in Chicago's Iroquois Theatre fire.

March Amphidrome by Conrad Sagemiller (City of Houghton Ralph Raffaelli Collection)

Portage Lake had an outstanding season but local fans wanted to see their team play the very best teams from Canada. It was not entertaining to see their club beat others teams by scores of 24-0 or 20-0, and if teams would not come to Houghton to play, perhaps Houghton would need to join a league that would provide better competition and more exciting games for the fans.

Following the success of Portage Lake, and as the interest in hockey in the United States was growing, Dee wrote Arthur McSwigan and others from the Western Pennsylvania Hockey League about forming a national hockey association or league with up to a dozen teams. Dee indicated that based on his experience with the Portage Lake team, hockey could be a viable business venture and suggested that teams from Canada would be interested. Meetings were held in the summer and fall of 1904 as several business leaders expressed interest and were excited about the idea of a professional hockey league.

Gibson was always respected throughout the Copper Country and was involved in numerous events and activities. He played baseball and served as a referee for local hockey games and was an umpire for charity baseball games. He organized and played on a cricket team, and played on a Portage Lake football team. He curled and in March 1904 he organized a team of Portage Lake hockey players to challenge a team from the Portage Lake Curling Club. In addition to Gibson, the team included Hod Stuart, Bert Morrison, and Riley Hern as the skip. Doc Gibson often served as the referee in local high school hockey games and Bruce Stuart was coach of the Houghton High School team.

Local high school hockey was first played in 1903 but was discontinued after a few seasons. High school hockey returned in the late 1920s but was again discontinued in the 1930s. It returned in 1969 with several teams and continues today.

Hancock Central High School Hockey Team, 1904
(Houghton County Historical Society)
Standing, left to right: *E.A. Meyers (manager), Will Waara (forward), Joe Linder (rover and captain), James Carrigan (point). Seated, left to right: John Steinbeck (forward), John Tamblyn (cover point), Albert Black (spare), Ed Reid (goal). In foreground, left to right: George Linder (forward), Earl Guibault (spare)*

Hancock defeated Houghton for the 1904 league championship and Amphidrome Cup. The trophy is displayed in the photograph. Joe Linder was the best player on the HCH hockey team and an outstanding football and baseball player. He was recruited as a spare for three games with the 1903–04 Portage Lake hockey team. Linder was inducted into the United States Hockey Hall of Fame in 1975. Another player on the team was Albert Black. Black is believed to be the first black high school hockey player in the United States.

Portage Lake Football Team (City of Houghton Ralph Raffaelli Collection)

Red Jacket Fat Men's Baseball Team, 1904 (Houghton County Historical Society) Standing, left to right: *Elmer Oleson (right field), Jack Dunn (second base), Billie Wills (first base), Ed Merz (shortstop, left field, and captain), Lanning Lewis (center field), Vic Barquist (left field)*. Seated, left to right: *Butch Kemp (catcher), Dr. Charles Rupprecht (manager), Charles Annen (short stop)*. In foreground, left to right: *Neil Kelly (third base), James Foulkes (pitcher)*

Gibson played for the Portage Lake football team that included Herman Gundlach Sr. and Dr. Harkness, Dr. Hay, and Dr. Willson. Gibson is third from the left in the middle row and Gundlach is in the black and white striped sweater in the middle row. Gundlach was a contractor and among his local projects included the Douglass House expansion and many of the original buildings on the Michigan College of Mines (Michigan Tech) campus

Baseball was a popular summer sport in the Copper Country and one the major attractions was the Red Jacket Fat Men's team. The team would play the Laurium Fat Men's team a few times during the summer as charity events and Gibson would be the umpire. The manager of the Laurium team was James T. Fisher who would later serve on the International Hockey League executive committee. The two teams also played charity hockey games and Gibson was the referee.

LIFE IN 1904

- The population of the United States was 82 million and the five largest U.S. cities were New York, Chicago, Philadelphia, St. Louis, and Boston.

- The population of Michigan was 2.5 million and Michigan's largest city was Detroit with a population of 300,000—the thirteenth largest city in the U.S. The population of Houghton County was 70,000.

- The population of Canada was 6 million and the largest cities in Canada were Montreal, Toronto, Quebec City, and Ottawa.

- The average life expectancy was 47 years and the five leading causes of death were pneumonia and influenza, tuberculosis, diarrhea, heart disease, and stroke.

- The average worker typically worked a 60 hour week and would earn $400–$600 per year. Teachers would average $325 per year, accountants $2,000 per year, dentists about $2,500 per year, veterinarians $4,000 per year, and engineers could earn close to $5,000 per year.

- Almost 90% of all doctors had no college degree. Many medical schools operated as profit-making "diploma mills" and there were no standards or government regulations for a medical degree with the result that the caliber of doctors varied greatly from very able and caring individuals to quacks.

- More than 95% of all births took place in the home and most women did not reveal that they were expecting a child.

- About 20% of adults could not read or write and only 6% of all Americans graduated from high school.

- Only 14% of the homes had a bathtub, about 8% of the homes had a telephone, and 18% of households had at least one full-time servant or domestic.

- The most popular leisure time activities were family get-togethers, picnics, and baseball. Skating and hockey were popular winter sports in the Copper Country.

- Marijuana, heroin, and morphine were all available over the counter at neighborhood drugstores and Coca Cola contained cocaine.

- The railroad was the predominant transportation mode for intercity travel and there were over 200,000 miles of railroad tracks in the U.S. and over 720 million annual rail passengers. There were 55,000 registered automobiles and few paved roads. Walking, bicycles, horse and buggies and sleighs were the common means of transportation in small towns and streetcars were popular in larger towns and cities. There were over 20 million horses in the United States.

- There were only 230 murders in the entire country.

- There was no federal income tax.

EVENTS OF 1904

Theodore Roosevelt was the U.S. President. He became President in 1901 following the assassination of William McKinley and won his first election in 1904.

The U.S. gained control of the Panama Canal Zone and a team of U.S. Army engineers began construction of the Panama Canal in May 1904.

The Wright Brothers made their initial flights in December 1903 at Kitty Hawk, NC and returned to Dayton for further testing and development throughout 1904.

The first New Year's Eve celebration was held in Times Square, New York City, on December 31, 1904.

President Roosevelt
(Library of Congress)

The Louisiana Purchase Exposition World's Fair was held in St. Louis (April 30–December 1, 1904) and several foods are claimed to have been introduced at the Fair—ice cream cones, the hot dog, Dr. Pepper.

St. Louis World's Fair (Library of Congress)

Games of the III Olympiad (Summer Olympics) were also held in St. Louis as part of the World's Fair (July 1–November 23).

The Boston Americans were the American Baseball League champions and the National League champion was the New York Giants but they refused to participate in the 1904 World Series. The first World Series was held in 1903 and Boston defeated Pittsburgh for the championship.

The college football national championship was shared by the Michigan Wolverines, Minnesota Golden Gophers, and Penn Quakers. In response to repeated deaths and injuries in college football, President Roosevelt organized meetings in 1905 which lead to the establishment of the forerunner of the National Collegiate Athletic Association (NCAA).

The Ottawa Hockey Club (Silver Seven) won the Stanley Cup in January and were victorious in challenges by teams from Toronto and Brandon, Manitoba, during the year. In the summer of 1904, a challenge was made and accepted from Dawson City, Yukon for a two-game series that took place in Ottawa in January 1905

Advertisement for Spalding Hockey Sticks and Pucks (Spalding)

Advertisement in Houghton Daily Mining Gazette, March 1904

CHAPTER 5
The Original International Hockey League

New League Organized

Following months of discussion, James Dee organized an initial meeting in August 1904 with representatives from Pittsburgh, Sault Ste. Marie, Michigan, and the Copper Country. The meeting was held in Detroit to determine the interest and prospects of organizing a league that would be known as the "American Hockey League." Business leaders from several cities including Chicago, Cleveland, Detroit, Duluth, Grand Rapids, Minneapolis, Milwaukee, Montreal, New York, St. Louis, and St. Paul expressed interest in a franchise but they decided not to proceed at that time. A group from Sault Ste. Marie, Ontario was also interested and indicated they would attend the next meeting. In early November 1904, representatives from Calumet, Houghton (Portage Lake), Pittsburgh, Sault Ste. Marie, Michigan, and Sault Ste. Marie, Ontario met in Chicago and agreed to form a professional hockey league. They adopted the name "International Hockey League (IHL)." It would be the first professional hockey league in which all players would be openly paid to pay hockey. The attendees at the meeting and the cities that they represented were:

Calumet—Charles Thompson, Laurium Agent for the Copper Range Railroad

Pittsburgh—Arthur L. McSwiggan, President, Duquesne Gardens

Portage Lake (Houghton)—James R. Dee, President, Amphidrome

Sault Ste. Marie, Michigan (Michigan Soo)—A.D. Ferguson, Manager, Soo Curling Club

Sault Ste. Marie, Ontario (Canadian Soo)—J.C. Boyd, Superintendent, Canadian Ship Canal

A.L. McSwiggan was elected League President, A.D. Ferguson was elected Vice President, and James Dee was elected for the important position of Secretary-Treasurer.

It was agreed that each of the five teams would play a 24 game schedule with three home games and three away games against each of the other teams. A revenue sharing plan, as proposed by the Canadian Soo group, was adopted in which the gate receipts would be divided 60% for the home team and 40% for the visiting team, with a minimum guarantee for the visiting team. The members felt that revenue sharing would make the long journey to Pittsburgh more attractive given that the potential gate generated in Pittsburgh's Duquesne Gardens would be larger due to a larger seating capacity.

The executive prepared a set of league operating rules and rules that would govern play. At the time, there were several versions of rules, such as the Ontario Hockey Association (OHA), the Canadian Amateur Hockey League, the American Amateur Hockey League

Rules, and others that were used in different regions of Canada and the United States. The League chose to adopt the "Quebec Rules." The major difference between the OHA rules and the Quebec rules was in the interpretation of off-side. Under the OHA rules, a player could pass the puck forward to a teammate as long as he skated quickly ahead so that he was ahead of the player that received the pass by time the puck reached his teammate. Under the Quebec rules, passes could not, under any circumstances, be made towards the opposing goal. Players would carry the puck into the opposition end on the rink and pass back to a teammate. It was felt that the Quebec rules were more conducive to team play which would make the games more spectacular. The acquisition of players for the league would be the sole responsibility of the individual teams, and managers soon began contacting the best players in Canada, building their rosters to begin play in December.

The five franchises in hockey's first professional hockey league were:
- **Calumet**, Michigan
- **Pittsburgh**, Pennsylvania
- **Portage Lake** (Houghton, Michigan)
- **Sault Ste. Marie**, Michigan (Michigan Soo)
- **Sault Ste. Marie**, Ontario (Canadian Soo).

International Hockey League Operating Rules

(from *Houghton Daily Mining Gazette*, December 15, 1904)

Section 1. The season shall be from the first of December to the 15th day of March, both days inclusive.

Section 2. The championship shall be decided by a series of games, a schedule of which shall be drawn up by one delegate from each club or company at the annual meeting. The club winning the most matches will be declared champions.

Section 3. All championship matches shall be played on rinks arranged for by the home club, subject to the jurisdiction of the league.

Section 4. The league shall offer a championship trophy to the winning club, to hold same and be recognized as champions of the league. The trophy shall be delivered to the winning club within ten days after the close of the season.

Section 5. Any club holding the trophy for three years in succession shall become absolute owners of the trophy.

Section 6. Any team making default shall forfeit the right to compete for the championship for that season, and will be required to pay the opposing team (within ten days), a fine of $300, unless a previous notice of ten days be given to the opposing team and to the league of such club's intention to default. Such notice must be in writing, and signed by the president and manager of the defaulting club or company. All matches played with defaulting clubs shall count, and previous matches awarded to opposing clubs.

Section 7. It shall be the duty of the captains of the contesting teams to hand to the referee the names of the players for each previous to the start, on forms supplied by the secretary of the league. The referee shall fill in the date of the match, names of the contesting clubs, the score at the finish, with names of umpires and timekeepers the whole duty signed by himself and forwarded to the secretary of the league.

Rules Governing Play in the International Hockey League

Section 1. A team shall be comprised of seven players, who shall be bonafide members of the club or company they represent. No player shall be allowed to play on more than one team in the same series during the season except with the consent of the holding club.

Section 2. The game shall be commenced and renewed by a face in the center of the rink. Ice surface must be at least 150 feet long by 50 feet wide. Goals shall be six feet wide and four feet high, and provided with goals nets, such as approved by the league. The goals shall be placed at least eight feet from the edge of the ice.

NOTE: *A face is a "face-off" in today's hockey terminology. The puck was placed by the sticks of two opponents, and then the referee who call "play." It was a few later years before referees adopted the practice of dropping the puck.*

Section 3. Two 30 minute halves or periods (running time), with an intermission of ten minutes between, will be the time allowed for matches, but no stops of more than five minutes will be allowed. A match will be decided by the team winning the greatest number of goals during that time. In case of a tie after playing the specified two halves, ten minutes shall be allowed. Ends will be changed and play will continue until one side secures a goal, but in no case shall the extra time exceed fifteen minutes. In the event of no deciding goal being secured by either team, the referee shall declare the match a draw, the game shall be played out the following night or the next open date, unless otherwise agreed to by the managers of the two teams. All matches shall start at the advertised time, and if for any reason there be more than fifteen minutes delay in the commencement of the match, the club at fault shall play to the league, as a penalty, the sum of $250, unless good reason be given for said delay. The referee is to see that this rule is observed, and to notify the league within two days should any breach of it occur.

Section 4. No change of players shall be made after a match commenced except for reasons of accidents or injury during the game.

Section 5. Should any player be injured during the first half of the match and compelled to leave the ice, his side shall be allowed to put on a spare man from the reserve to equalize the team. Should any player be injured during the second half of the match, the captain of the opposing team shall have the option of dropping a player to equalize the team, or allow the opponent to put on a man from the reserve. In the event of any dispute between the captains as to the injured player's fitness to continue the game, the matter shall at once be decided by the referee.

Section 6. Should the game be temporarily stopped by the infringement of any of the rules, the captain of the opposite team may claim that the puck be taken back and face take place where it was last played before the infringement occurred.

Section 7. When the player hits the puck, anyone on the same side, who at such moment of hitting is nearer the opponent's goal line is out of play, and may not touch the puck himself or in any way prevent any other player from doing so, until the puck has been played. A player must always be on his own side of the puck.

Section 8. The puck may be stopped, but not carried or knocked on by any part of the body, nor shall any player close his hand or carry the puck to the ice in his hand. No player shall raise his stick above the shoulder except in lifting the puck. Charging from behind, cross checking, tripping, collaring, kicking, clubbing or slashing shall not be allowed, and for any infringement of these rules, the referee may rule the offending player off the ice for that match or for portion of actual playing time as he may see fit. Should any player be ruled off the ice for time more than once during a match, the referee shall penalize him for each succeeding offense not less than twice the period of time penalized for his preceding offense.

Section 9. When the puck goes off the ice or a foul occurs between the goals, it should be taken by the referee to five yards from the goal line and then faced. When the puck goes off the ice at the sides, it shall be taken by the referee to five yards at right angles from the boundary line and there faced.

Section 10. The goal keeper must not during play, lie, kneel or sit upon the ice, but must maintain a standing position. For infringement of this section the referee shall have the authority to rule the offending player off the ice for that match or for such portion of actual playing time as he may see fit.

Section 11. Goal shall be scored when the puck shall have passed between the goal posts in front below an imaginary line across the tops of the posts.

Section 12. Hockey sticks shall not be more than three inches wide at any point.

Section 13. The puck must be made of rubber, one inch thick all through and three inches in diameter. The Spalding hockey puck, the official puck of the league, must be used in all matches, the home team to furnish the referee with a puck previous to the match.

Section 14. All disputes during the match shall be decided by the referee, and he shall have full control of all players and officials from the commencement to finish of matches, inclusive of stops and his decisions shall be final.

Section 15. All questions as to goals shall be settled by the umpires and their decisions shall be final.

Section 16. In the event of any dispute as to the decision of an umpire or timekeeper, the referee shall have the power to remove and replace him.

Section 17. Any player guilty of using profane or abusive language to any spectator, officials or other players shall be liable to be ruled off by the referee, as per Section 8.

Section 18. Any claims or contentions regarding the plays or interpretation of rules shall be made by the captains only.

Calumet, Michigan

Calumet is an area located about ten miles north of Houghton that included Red Jacket, Laurium, and several mining towns. It was the home of the Calumet and Hecla Mining Company, the largest copper mining company in the area and the population of the Calumet area in 1904 approached 35,000. Red Jacket was the commercial and social center of the area and Laurium was primarily a residential area with many large homes and mansions for merchants, bankers, and mining managers and executives. The Copper Range Railroad and Mineral Range Railroad provided excellent passenger and freight service for the area and streetcar service linking Houghton/Hancock with Red Jacket, Laurium, and Wolverine began in 1901. A branch line to Lake Linden and Hubbell opened in the summer of 1903. Businessmen in Calumet were excited by the success of the Portage Lake hockey team and felt that a Calumet team would be successful but they realized that a new hockey arena would be needed. Under the leadership of Johnson Vivian Jr., the Laurium Storage and Warehouse Company was formed to build a large arena. Vivian operated a large department store, was president of the State Savings Bank in Laurium, and was active in several local affairs including the promotion of horse racing, curling, and hockey. The new arena was built in the fall of 1904 in Laurium on the corner of Isle Royale and Third Streets, adjacent to the Copper Range Railroad depot and a few blocks from the Houghton County streetcar line that operated on Hecla Street, through downtown Laurium. It was built by the Wisconsin Bridge and Iron Company and C.A. Anderson at a cost of $25,000, and had a seating capacity for 3,000 spectators and a natural ice surface of 180 feet by 78 feet. A local woman won a naming contest and the arena would be known as the Palestra.

While the Palestra was under construction, former Portage Lake star player, Hod Stuart was hired as manager of the Palestra and captain of the Calumet team. He was paid $1800 for his many duties and quickly began recruiting players for the team. Although teams in the league did not have formal nicknames, the press would often give them names in newspaper stories. The Calumet team was called the "Miners," the "Wanderers," or the "Calumets" and they wore pearl gray and cardinal red sweaters.

Fifth Street was the main shopping street in downtown Red Jacket. This photograph was taken at the corner of Fifth Street and Pine Street. The Calumet area included Red Jacket, Laurium, and several mining communities and the population in 1904 approached 35,000. (Michigan Technological University Archives and Copper Country Historical Collections)

Calumet sweater (SIHR Sweater Museum)

The Palestra was the home of the Calumet IHL team. The arena was located on the corner of Third Street and Isle Royale in Laurium and opened in December 1904.

(Michigan Technological University Archives and Copper Country Historical Collections)

The Palestra had a seating capacity of 3,000 and a natural ice surface of 180 feet by 78 feet. (City of Houghton Ralph Raffaelli Collection)

Pittsburgh, Pennsylvania

Pittsburgh was the largest city in the league with a 1904 population of over 320,000—it was the eleventh largest city in the United States at the time. Pittsburgh grew rapidly during the decade as immigrants arrived seeking one of the many factory jobs in this major industrial city. In 1910 the population of Pittsburgh was over 530,000. Steel production began in Pittsburgh in the 1870s when Andrew Carnegie founded the Carnegie Steel Company and when Carnegie sold his steel plants to J.P. Morgan in 1901, Carnegie became one of the world's richest men. Within a few years, over half of the nation's steel was produced in Pittsburgh, "The Steel City." Other industrialists in Pittsburgh during this era included Andrew W. Mellon (aluminum, banking), George Westinghouse (Westinghouse Electric), Charles Schwab (investment banking), and Henry Heinz (food).

The Copper Range Railroad Depot was adjacent to the Palestra and special service was available for hockey fans. (Michigan Technological University Archives and Copper Country Historical Collections)

Pittsburgh was the largest city in the league with a 1904 population of over 320,000. It grew rapidly during the decade with the development of numerous industries. (Library of Congress Detroit Publishing Collection)

CHAPTER 5: THE ORIGINAL INTERNATIONAL HOCKEY LEAGUE ● 71

A photograph of downtown Pittsburgh in the early 1900s. The Steel City was the home to several famous industrialists including Andrew Carnegie, J.P. Morgan, Andrew mellon, George Westinghouse, Charles Schwab, and Henry Heinz (Library of Congress Detroit Publishing Company)

With the opening of the Duquesne Gardens and subsequent formation of the Western Pennsylvania Hockey League (WPHL) in 1901, hockey was very popular. The WPHL had four teams—the Pittsburgh Bankers, the Pittsburgh Victorias, the Pittsburgh Keystones, and the Pittsburgh Athletic Club—all games were played at the 5,000 seat Duquesne Gardens. The league attracted the top players from Canada with the promise of high paying jobs in the Pittsburgh area and small weekly cash incentives ($10–$15) to play on one of the teams. The manager for each team was paid a lump sum to pay his players and the less money that the manager had to pay them, the more money the manager got to keep. Many have considered these players to be semi-professional as the primary attraction to Pittsburgh was jobs. When the IHL began operations in 1904, the WPHL suspended the league and the best players joined the Pittsburgh team or one of the other four league teams. Over half of the players in the IHL had played in Pittsburgh at one time. The Pittsburgh team was known as the "Pros," "Professionals," or the "Coal Heavers" and their colors were red and blue.

An interesting note of this era is the spelling of Pittsburgh. Pittsburgh was chartered as a city in 1816 and is one of the few American cities to be spelled with an "h" at the end of the "burg" suffix. In 1890, the United States Board of Geographic Names decided that the "h" was to be dropped in the names of all cities and towns ending in "burg." However in 1911, following a protest from citizens who wished to preserve the historic spelling, the Board reversed its decision and restored the "h" to Pittsburgh, but for the twenty year period, confusion and controversy was common and one would see both spellings—"Pittsburg" and "Pittsburgh."

Pittsburgh sweater (SIHR Sweater Museum)

Portage Lake (Houghton), Michigan

The Portage Lake team was probably the most prepared for the league. The team won the U.S. Championship and World Championship in March 1904 and was well-versed in recruiting and paying the best players from Canada. James Dee and Gibson were the prime movers for the new professional hockey league and the Amphidrome was one of the finest arenas in the country. Several renovations were completed at the Amphidrome in the fall as a new home team dressing room was added and improvements were made in the lobby area. Although the 1904 population for Houghton-Hancock was about 10,000 (Houghton 4,000 and Hancock 6,000), the local fans provided enthusiastic support for the team and were excited by the prospective for better competition. Dee continued in his role as team President and John McNamara was named manager for the team. McNamara was the Houghton County sheriff and manager of the Amphidrome. The Portage Lake team continued to wear their green and white sweaters and although the team did not have a formal name, the press would often refer to them as the "Lakes" or "Lakers."

The Houghton waterfront with a new Portage Bridge connecting Houghton and Hancock. In 1904 Houghton had a population of about 4,000 and Hancock's population was about 6,000. (Michigan Technological University Archives and Copper Country Historical Collections)

Portage Lake sweater (SIHR Sweater Museum)

Downtown Houghton in the early 1900s. Note the eastbound streetcar on Shelden Avenue and the famous Douglass House hotel in the center of the photograph. (Michigan Technological University Archives and Copper Country Historical Collections)

Sault Ste. Marie, Michigan (Michigan Soo)

Sault Ste. Marie, Michigan lies on the eastern end of Michigan's Upper Peninsula on the Canadian border and is separated from Sault Ste. Marie, Ontario by the St. Mary's River. The area was originally inhabited by several Indian tribes as a gathering place for fishing, hunting, and trapping. It became the first European settlement in the late 1600s when Father Jacques Marquette established a Catholic mission, and grew quickly as an important trade route between Lake Superior and the other Great Lakes. Sault Ste. Marie is the oldest settlement in Michigan and one of the oldest cities in the United States. The rapids on the St. Mary's River were a choke point for shipping as early ships portaged around the rapids in a process that would take weeks as cargoes were unloaded, hauled around the rapids, and then loaded unto other ships waiting below the rapids. The first American lock was built in 1855 and this was instrumental in improving shipping on the Great Lakes and opening markets for Upper Peninsula iron ore and copper. In 1903, a water power canal and house were completed to provide cheaper electricity for several new industries that located in the city. This was a booming and prosperous time. The city's name Sault Sainte Marie, translates from the French as the "Rapids of the Saint Mary", and is usually written as Sault Ste. Marie but often referred to as the "Sault" or the "Soo." In 1904 the population of the Michigan Soo was about 11,500 and was linked to Sault Ste. Marie, Ontario with frequent ferry service across the St. Mary's River. The Duluth, South Shore, and Atlantic Railroad (DSS&A) provided rail service across the Upper Peninsula with connections to other railroads serving Chicago and the Minneapolis-St. Paul area.

Because of its proximity to Sault Canada, hockey was a popular game as local teams would compete at the amateur level with teams from Sault Canada, other communities in Northern Ontario, and the Copper Country in the early 1900s. When Portage Lake began to pay players for the 1903–04 season, Michigan Soo begin paying players and scheduled games with Portage Lake, and Sault Canada. The team played in the Ridge Street Ice-A-Torium on Ridge

Sault Ste. Marie, Michigan and Sault Ste. Marie, Ontario are separated by the St. Mary's River. The rapids on the St. Mary's River provided a challenge to early shipping as cargoes were unloaded, hauled around the rapids, and then loaded on waiting ships. The name Sault Sainte Marie translates from the French as the "Rapids of the Saint Mary." (Library of Congress Detroit Publishing Collection)

The first American lock opened in 1855 and made it more cost effective for the shipping of Upper Peninsula iron ore and copper to the Chicago and Detroit markets. This photograph was taken in the early 1900s and shows ships passing through the Soo Locks. The Weitzel Lock is on the left and it was replaced by the MacArthur Lock in 1943. The first Poe Lock is on the right; it was built in 1896 and rebuilt with the same name in 1968. Lake Superior is located in the distance or top of the photograph. (Library of Congress Detroit Publishing Collection)

Street, near Ferris Street, next to the Iroquois Hotel and Soo Locks. The building was originally a curling rink so there were challenges with obstructions for spectators to view the whole ice surface and management diligently worked to remedy the problems. The press referred to the team as the "Indians" or the "Wolverines" and team colors were purple and white.

The arena for the Michigan Soo IHL team was the Ridge Street Ice-A-Torium. It was located on Ridge Street, near Ferris Street, and next to the Soo Locks Canal Park. The arena is the barn structure in the center of the photograph. The building next to the arena was the Iroquois Hotel. The hotel was destroyed in a 1907 fire. (Library of Congress Detroit Publishing Collection)

1905 was the 50th Anniversary of the opening of the Soo Locks. This photograph shows a celebration parade on Ashman Street, the main street of Sault Michigan. The population of Sault Michigan at the time was about 11,500. (Library of Congress Detroit Publishing Collection)

Michigan Soo sweaters
Bottom: 1904–05 sweater
Top: 1905–06 and 1906–07 sweater
(SIHR Sweater Museum)

Sault Ste. Marie, Ontario (Canadian Soo)

Sault Ste. Marie, Ontario was incorporated as a town in 1887 and a Canadian Ship Canal (Lock) was completed in 1895 to provide for easier passage of Canadian ships. One of the early entrepreneurs was industrialist Frances Clergue who founded and developed several companies including power companies, a pulp and paper mill, the International Transit Company (a streetcar and ferry company), Algoma Steel (opened in 1902), and the Algoma Central Railroad. The early 1900s were an exciting time in the Sault, and in the ten year period from 1900 to 1910, the population grew from 4,000 to 11,000. When the IHL began in 1904, the population was about 6,000 making it the smallest town in the league. As Canada's game, hockey was well established in the community with several teams and leagues. Sault teams would play against teams from Michigan and other Ontario towns, but the cost of travel was always a challenge. When they played Michigan Soo or Portage Lake teams during the 1903–04 season, the OHA expressed concerns and threatened expulsion from the Association. If you were playing professional teams, your team was suspected of being a professional team too.

The Canadian Soo team played their home games in the Soo Curling Club's Gouin Street Arena, located between Queen and Bay

The main street in Sault Ontario was Queen Street. In this winter photograph, one is looking west on Queen Street at East Street and to the bottom right is the location of the Gouin Street Arena, home of the Canadian Soo team. In 1904, the population of Sault Ontario was about 6,000 making it the smallest town in the league. The early 1900s were an exciting time of growth and development in the Sault and by 1910, the two Saults had about the same population (Government of Canada Library and Archives)

Streets near East Street. The arena had a seating capacity of about 1,000 for a hockey game. The team was known as the "Marlboros" and the "Algonquins" and its colors were initially red and black and then changed to red and white in the team's second season.

The Canadian Soo Locks opened in 1895 to provide passage for Canadian ships. Note the bridge in the distance for freight railroad traffic. (Government of Canada Library and Archives)

Canadian Soo sweaters
Bottom: *1904–05 sweater.* Top: *1905–06 and 1906–07 sweater.* (SIHR Sweater Museum)

CHAPTER 6
Three Seasons of Professional Hockey

The First Season 1904–05

Following the decision to establish the International Hockey League, team managers moved quickly to assemble line-ups and put together a schedule for the 1904–05 season. Each team played a 24 game schedule with three home games and three away games against each of the other teams. It was often a challenge to schedule games to avoid conflicts with other events in the community.

Portage Lake retained Riley Hern, Doc Gibson, Bruce Stuart, Bert Morrison, and "Cooney" Shields from the 1903–04 championship team, but lost Hod Stuart to the new Calumet team as manager of the Palestra and captain of the Calumet team. The Portage Lake team brought back Fred Lake from Sault Michigan and added Barney Holden from Winnipeg, Harry Bright from Montreal, and Charlie Liffiton from Pittsburgh.

In Calumet, Hod Stuart realized that he needed a strong team to compete with Portage Lake, so he imported Jimmy Gardner, Ken Mallen, Bill Nicholson, and Fred Strike from the Montreal Wanderers and added Robert "Doc" Scott from Queen's University and Aenas "Red" McMillan from Cornwall.

In Sault Michigan, manager Joe Stephens recruited James Robinson from Kingston, Eddie Howell from Paris, Ontario, and two stars from Montreal—Jack Laviolette and Diedre Pitre—to join Chief Jones, Frank Switzer, and Billy Hamilton from the 1903–04 Sault team.

In Sault Ontario, Roy Brown from Paris and OHA fame was hired to manage the new team, and he recruited several Brantford players including Billy "Lady" Taylor, Frank Clifton, and Edward Gillard, along with Charles Collins from Collingwood, Pete Maltman from Woodstock, and Dick O'Leary and Garnet Sixsmith from Ottawa.

In Pittsburgh, Charlie Spittal of Ottawa was put in charge and he recruited the best players from the four Pittsburgh teams in the Western Pennsylvania Hockey League. The players included Billy Duval, Alwyn Kent, James MacKay, and Ed Roberts from Ottawa, Lorne Campbell and Tom Melville from Montreal, and Haddo Black from Windsor.

The first IHL game was played on Friday, December 9, 1904 at the Duquesne Gardens in Pittsburgh. Nearly 4,000 fans attended and saw Portage Lake's Barney Holden score the first goal as Portage Lake defeated Pittsburgh 6-3. The first game in Sault, Michigan was played on December 14 between the two Sault teams and the first game played in Sault, Ontario was on December 19 when the two Sault teams met in a return match. The first game in the Copper Country was played at the new Palestra on Friday, December 16. Calumet defeated Portage Lake 4-3 and beat them again 4-1 in a rematch on the next night in the Houghton Amphidrome.

Teams would often make several line-up changes during the season due to injuries or other commitments. Players discovered their

Portage Lake's Barney Holden scored the first goal in the first IHL game (Daniel Holden Collection)

HOUGHTON WON HOCKEY GAME

Visitors Shot Six Goals to Locals' Three in a Hard Contest

Portage Lake opened the local hockey season last night at Duquesne Garden by winning from the Pittsburg team, 6 to 3. During the first half the Houghton seven ran away from Pittsburg by scoring four goals, the locals drawing a blank. The second half was more productive for the Pittsburg, and they negotiated three goals, while the visitors added two more to their count.

Fred Lake got a hard fall during the game and it was fully three minutes before the plucky little fellow could resume play.

There were several minor accidents during the contest, but none of the players was seriously hurt. Eddie Roberts was cut over the eye in a collision with Holden; Bill Shields got a slight cut on the arm and Bruce Stuart was kicked on the leg with a skate, which made him jump for a moment.

Goalkeeper Mackay was penalized for two minutes for going down on his knees in front of his goal to block shots at his net. There were a number of penalties for violations of the rules.

Holden shot the first goal for Portage Lake on a pass from Shields, who made a long run. Shields shot the second goal from the side of the rink, digging the disc from a scrimmage. Lake scored the third for the visitors from scrimmage and Bruce Stuart registered the fourth before the end of the first period on a pass from Holden.

Pittsburg registered their first goal in the second half on a run by Spittal, who passed to Black, the latter passing to Campbell, who made the shot. Garnet Sixsmith shot the second goal on a pass from Roberts. Then Portage Lake cut in with another score, Shields making the shot. Lake and Gibson took the disc for a long run, Gibson making the sixth and final goal for the visitors.

Duval got another goal for Pittsburg before the end of the period by lifting the disc into the net from the center of the rink after about a dozen trials.

Line-up:

Portage Lake—6.		Pittsburg—3.
Hern	Goal	Mackay
Gibson	Point	Spittal
Holden	Cover point	Duval
Morrison	Forward	Roberts
Stuart	Center	Campbell
Shields	Right wing	Black
Lake	Left wing	Sixsmith

Goals—Gibson, Holden, Stuart, Shields 2, Lake, Duval, Campbell, Sixsmith. Referee—Schooley.

The First IHL Game, Pittsburg Press, December 10, 1904

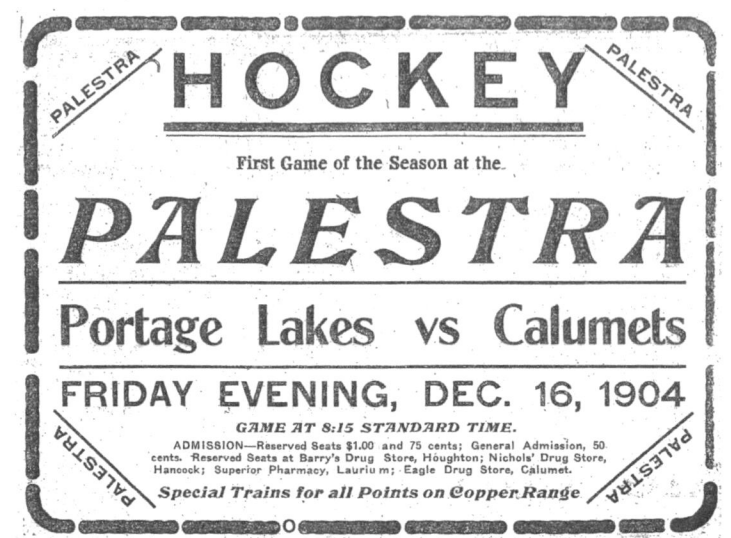

Advertisement in Calumet News, *December 14, 1904.*

The Palestra in Laurium (Keweenaw National Historical Park)

Look! Listen! Think!

In the sporting line, don't forget the GREAT HOCKEY GAME at the Palestra Friday night, Dec. 16.

IT'S AN ASSURED FACT

The Copper Range Railroad will run a special train to accomodate the South Range, Houghton, Hancock Dollar Bay and Lake Linden Hockeyites.

Train leaves Painesdale 6:30 p. m.; Trimountain 6:33 South Range 6:37, Atlantic 6.48, Houghton 7.00, Hancock 7:05 stopping at all intermediate stations. Returning at the close of the game. Accomodations on this special for ONLY 1000 people so hurry and avoid the rush.

ONE FARE FOR THE ROUND TRIP

This will be the greatest Hockey Game ever played in the Copper Country. DON'T MISS IT.

REMEMBER THE DATE
FRIDAY, DECEMBER 16th, 1904.

Advertisement in Calumet News, *December 14, 1904.*

AMPHIDROME
HOCKEY
TONIGHT
Calumet vs. Portage Lake

Well you see what the results were last night and tonight will be the greatest game ever seen in the Copper Country.

DONT MISS THIS GAME

Reserved seats on sale at Barry's, Houghton, Nichols, Hancock, Eagle Drug Store, Calumet, Superior Drug Store, Laurium.

SPECIAL TRAIN ON COPPER RANGE

Painesdale and all intermediate stations on regular train leaving Painesdale at 6.30 p. m. returning after the game, one fare for the round trip. Calumet and intermediate stations on regular train leaving Calumet at 7 p. m. returning after the game. One fare for the round trip. Game starts at 9.00 sharp.

Advertisement in Calumet News, *December 17, 1904.*

Streetcar in a snow storm in Red Jacket but note the advertisement for upcoming Pittsburg-Calumet games at the Palestra. (Michigan Technological University Archives and Copper Country Historical Collections)

value, sold their services to the highest bidder, and would move to a new team during the season as true free-agents. "Cooney" Shields quit Portage Lake to referee, but when Calumet's Robert Scott was injured Shields came out of retirement and completed the season with Calumet. Pittsburgh got off to a slow start giving up over six goals per game so they brought in a new goalie Jack Winchester from Bellville and Billy Baird from Ottawa. The Sault Ontario recruited Oliver Seibert from Berlin, but he broke his leg in his first game, and was out for the season. Since the Duquesne Gardens had artificial ice, Pittsburgh finished their schedule earlier than other teams and their players were free to join other teams in the league. Lorne Campbell, one of Pittsburgh's top players, joined Portage Lake for four games at the end of the season.

As the season began, most newspaper reporters felt that Portage Lake would dominate the league, but Hod Stuart had recruited an outstanding team and they won the league championship. The team was led by the league's two top goal scorers—Fred Strike and Ken Mallen—and the league's top goalie was Calumet's Billy Nicholson.

1904–05 IHL Final Standings

	GP	W	L	T	GF	GA	Pts
Calumet	24	18	5	1*	131	75	37
Portage Lake	24	15	7	2*	98	81	32
Michigan Soo	24	10	13	1	81	79	21
Pittsburgh	24	8	15	1	82	114	17
Canadian Soo	24	6	17	1	97	140	13

*A 1-1 tie played between Calumet and Portage Lake was officially awarded to Calumet due to Houghton's refusal to play overtime.

1904–05 League Top Goal Scorers

Fred Strike (Calumet)	44 goals
Ken Mallen (Calumet)	38
Bill Taylor (Canadian Soo)	35
Bruce Stuart (Portage Lake)	33
Lorne Campbell (Pittsburgh)	29

1904–05 Top Goalies (Goals Against Average)

Billy Nicholson (Calumet)	3.17
Chief Jones (Michigan Soo)	3.32
Riley Hern (Portage Lake)	3.54

1904–05 Penalty Minute Leaders

Bruce Stuart (Portage Lake)	59 minutes
Bob Scott (Calumet)	50
Jack Gibson (Portage Lake)	49

Portage Lake's top goal scorer was Bruce Stuart and he was the league leader in penalty minutes.

1904–05 Portage Lake Team

	Games Played	Goals
Bruce Stuart	22	33
Fred Lake	24	14
Bert Morrison	12	10
Henry Bright	8	9
Barney Holden	24	9
Charlie Liffiton	14	6
Cooney Shields	10	7
(played part of season for Calumet)		
Lorne Campbell	4	6
Jack "Doc" Gibson	24	2
Jack McMaster	1	
Ernie Westcott	3	0
Andy Haller	1	0

Goalie: Riley Hern 24 (2 shutouts) GAA: 3.54

As the season ended, Gibson announced that he was retiring as a hockey player. In recognition and appreciation of his service, James Dee presented Gibson with a diamond ring at the last game of the season at the Amphidrome with the following address:

A number of friends who are admirers of the game of hockey take pleasure in presenting to you this package which accompanies this as a token of your efforts in introducing the game in the community and in bringing it to its present high standing and repute, both here and elsewhere in the United States. We regret your contemplated retirement from active participation in the sport and wish you all success in your future life.

Calumet Hockey Club of Laurium, 1904–05 International Hockey League Champion.
Standing, left to right: *Joe Ziehr (trainer), Charles Thompson (manager), "Red" McMillan, Hod Stuart, "Lal" Earls, Johnson Vivian (president)*
Center Row, left to right: *Robert "Doc" Scott, William Nicholson, Jimmy Gardner*
Front Row, left to right: *Fred Strike, Ken Mallen*
(Houghton County Historical Society)

The Second Season 1905–06

During the summer of 1905, James Dee resigned from his position on the IHL board and was replaced by J.C. Boyd from Sault, Ontario. A. Ferguson and A. MacSwiggan exchanged positions as president and vice-president.

Elected Officers—1905–06:
President: A. Ferguson, Soo Curling Club, Sault Ste. Marie, Michigan
Vice President: A.L. MacSwiggan, Manager, Duquesne Gardens, Pittsburgh
Secretary-Treasurer: J.C. Boyd, Superintendent, Canadian Soo Ship Canal, Sault Ste. Marie, Ontario

In the first season, refereeing was the source of many complaints and disputes and it may have been justified as twenty different referees were used. For the second season the league decided to hire two referees. Doc Gibson retired from play and became a referee and Chaucer Elliott, acknowledged to be the best referee in Canada, was recruited for league games. The arrangement worked. A few teams questioned Gibson's allegiance to the Portage Lake team, but he was well respected and no serious problems developed.

Another concern following the first season was rising player salaries. Owners were concerned that they would lose money on their investment, so a team salary limit was set at $3,000. It may have helped to keep salaries low but during the season several accusations were made that teams were exceeding the limit. Since the hockey season lasted only a few months, players went home to their families and regular jobs in Canada at the end of each season. As a result team rosters would often change between seasons and it was a challenge for team managers to negotiate new contracts and recruit new players for each season.

Since Doc Gibson retired from play, Bruce Stuart took over the Portage Lake team's leadership role and Riley Hern, Barney Holden, Fred Lake, and Harry Bright returned for a second season. Grindy Forrester from Waterloo and Joe Hall from Brandon, Manitoba joined the team. Fred Taylor was added in mid-January and was paid $400 for six games and finished the season with the team.

In Calumet, the first year manager and star player, Hod Stuart, left Calumet following a salary dispute to play for Pittsburgh. He was replaced by Billy Shields. Billy Nicholson, Fred Strike, Ken Mallen, Jimmy Gardner, and Robert Scott returned from the championship team, but Mallen left early the team early in the season because of rough play and the team struggled during the season finishing fourth.

Jack Laviolette took over as manager of the Sault Michigan team and Chief Jones, Billy Hamilton, Ed Howell, Didier Pitre and Frank Switzer returned. Reddy McMillan moved over from the Calumet team. Pitre became a star and was the league's leading goal scorer.

Art Sixsmith was the new manager in Pittsburgh and despite the addition of Hod Stuart, strong scoring by Lorne Campbell and Sixsmith, and good goaltending by Billy Winchester, the team finished third.

Charlie Spittal became the manager in Sault, Ontario and brought in goalie Darcy Regan from Orillia. The team's star player Billy Taylor couldn't get along with Spittal, and the whole team was in chaos for most of the season. They folded in February and forfeited nine games to finish last in the league standings.

In a close race for the league's championship, Portage Lake finished first and Michigan Soo finished second. At the end of the season, there was talk of a game between Portage Lake and the Kenora Thistles who had just won the Manitoba League championship, but the Thistles declined for fear that a game would jeopardize their ability to challenge for the Stanley Cup. They were afraid that they would be seen as a professional team by the Stanley Cup trustees. Kenora did submit a challenge in the fall of 1906 and defeated the Montreal Wanderers in a two-game series in January 1907 to win the Stanley Cup. The Wanderers won their league championship in March 1907 and were able to challenge the Thistles for a return series in which the Wanderers won.

Portage Lake Hockey Team, 1905–06 International Hockey League Champion
Clockwise from top left: *Bruce Stuart (center and captain), Barney Holden (cover point), John McNamara (manager), Grindy Forrester (point), Joe Hall (right wing), Harry Bright (rover), James Duggan (trainer), Walter Forrest (spare), Fred Taylor (rover), Fred Lake (left wing)*
(Michigan Technological University Archives and Copper Country Historical Collections)

1905–06 IHL Final Standings

	GP	W	L	T	GF	GA	Pts
Portage Lake	24	19	5	0	105	70	38
Michigan Soo	24	18	6	0	126	57	36
Pittsburgh	24	15	9	0	121	84	30
Calumet	24	7	17	0	48	108	14
Canadian Soo*	24	1	23	0	56	137	2

*The Canadian Soo team disbanded during the season. In the official team standings, each game that was forfeited by the Canadian Soo team was awarded as a 1-0 victory for the opposing team. Nine games were forfeited.

1905–06 League Top Goal Scorers

Didier Pitre (Michigan Soo)	41 goals
Lorne Campbell (Pittsburgh)	35
Joe Hall (Portage Lake)	33
Fred Lake (Portage Lake)	25
Frank Schweitzer (Michigan Soo)	25

1905–06 Top Goalies (Goals Against Average)

Chief Jones (Michigan Soo)	2.55
Riley Hern (Portage Lake)	3.46
Billy Winchester (Pittsburgh)	3.52

1905–06 Penalty Minute Leaders

Joe Hall (Portage Lake)	98 minutes
Hod Stuart (Pittsburgh)	50
Cap McDonald (Calumet)	41

Joe Hall and Fred Lake were the top goal scorers for Portage Lake. The team played 20 games as four games with the Canadian Soo team were forfeited because the team disbanded before the season finished. Joe Hall was the league leader in penalty minutes.

1905–06 Portage Lake Team

	Games Played	Goals
Joe Hall	20	33
Fred Lake	20	25
Bruce Stuart	20	15
Fred Taylor	6	11
Barney Holden	20	9
Harry Bright	9	7
Grindy Forrester	20	4
Walter Forrest	5	0
Goalie: Riley Hern	20 (1 shutout) GAA 3.46	

The Third Season 1906–07

A new executive was elected for the 1906–07 season and the president was James Fisher representing the Calumet team. The executive realized that, in spite of league operating rules that a trophy be awarded to league champion, a trophy was never purchased. The league champion of the first two seasons received a pennant in recognition of their championship and it was not until the start of the third season that the executive talked about awarding a trophy. The names "Dee Cup" and "Ferguson Cup" were suggested but no further action was taken.

Elected Officers—1906–07:
President: James T. Fisher, Cashier, State Savings Bank, Laurium
Vice President: William L. Murdock, Manager, Northwest Leather Company, Sault Ste. Marie, Michigan
Secretary-Treasurer: John T. McNamara, Manager, Amphidrome, Houghton, Michigan

Bruce Stuart returned as captain of the Portage Lake team but goalie Riley Hern and high scoring Joe Hall returned to Canada. Hern joined the Montreal Wanderers and Hall joined his hometown Brandon Wheat Kings in the Manitoba Professional Hockey League. Fred Taylor, Barney Holden, Fred Lake, and Grindy Forrester returned and Stuart brought in Darcy Regan from the Canadian Soo team to play goalie and recruited George "Goldie" Cochrane from Berlin, Ontario. Gibson returned to play four games as a substitute during the season.

Billy Shields was back as captain in Calumet but the team lost Fred Strike and Jimmy Gardner, their leading players from previous teams. Strike joined the Ottawa team in Federal Amateur Hockey League and Jimmy Gardner joined the Pittsburgh team. Ken Mallen returned and Bert Morrison returned after a season with a Toronto team. Morrison led the team in goal scoring but the team struggled and finished last. The attendance at the Palestra dropped and quite often less than 500 fans were at a game as other community events became more attractive.

Jack Laviolette returned as the manager of the Michigan Soo team with virtually the same team that finished second in the previous season. He recruited Jack Ward from the Canadian Soo team and although it was a good team, they finished fourth in the final league standings. Didre Pitre led the team in scoring.

Pittsburgh was led by Hod Stuart and he recruited Tommy Smith, Jimmy Gardner, Horace Gaul, and Eddie Hogan. However when Stuart pulled his team off the ice in Michigan Soo to protest the decisions of referee Herman Meinke, Stuart was fired and replaced by Lorne Campbell. Stuart returned home to star for the Montreal Wanderers and the Pittsburgh team finished third.

After the Canadian Soo team disbanded during the previous season, owners wondered if the league could operate without the Canadian Soo team and during the fall the owners talked of renaming the league as the American Hockey League and expanding to other cities. Since the league was formed local newspapers would often report on league expansion and among the rumored cities included Buffalo, Chicago, Cleveland, Detroit, Duluth, Montreal, Milwaukee, Minneapolis, St. Paul, and Toronto. Toronto was actually awarded a franchise for the 1907–08 season.

The Canadian Soo team regrouped with new ownership. They lured Roy Brown back as manager and recruited several young stars including Hugh Lehman, Edouard "Newsy" Lalonde, Jack Marks, Harry McRobbie, and Marty Welsh. Billy Taylor was the team and league's top goal scorer and the team finished the season in second place.

Elliott and Gibson did not return as referees for the third season. Although Joe Stephens, former Michigan Soo manager, refereed 28 games, several referees were assigned during the season with the result that the problems and complaints about officiating of the first season again occurred.

In February, Pittsburgh inquired about a challenge for the Stanley Cup, but the trustees indicated that teams from the United States could not challenge for the Cup. The trustees said that if the Canadian Soo team won the league's championship they could challenge for the Cup, but the Canadian Soo team finished second to Portage Lake. With the Pittsburgh ruling in mind, Portage Lake did not submit a challenge.

1906–07 IHL Final Standings

	GP	W	L	T	GF	GA	Pts
Portage Lake	24	16	8	0	102	102	32
Canadian Soo	24	13	11	0	124	123	26
Pittsburgh	25	12	12	1	94	82	25
Michigan Soo	24	11	13	0	103	88	22
Calumet	25	8	16	1	96	124	17

1906–07 League Top Goal Scorers

Bill Taylor (Canadian Soo)	46 goals
Lorne Campbell (Pittsburgh)	35
Tommy Smith (Pittsburgh)	31
Newsy Lalonde (Canadian Soo)	29
Bert Morrison (Calumet)	28

1906–07 Top Goalies (Goals Against Average)

Billy Winchester (Pittsburgh)	3.40
Chief Jones (Michigan Soo)	3.80
Darcy Regan (Portage Lake)	4.36

1906–07 Penalty Minute Leaders

Bruce Stuart (Portage Lake)	81 minutes
Bob Scott (Calumet)	66
Jimmy Gardner (Pittsburgh)	61
Billy Hamilton (Michigan Soo)	61

1906–07 Portage Lake Team

	Games Played	Goals
Fred Lake	23	27
Bruce Stuart	23	20
Grindy Forrester	22	15
Fred Taylor	23	18
Goldie Cochrane	17	15
Barney Holden	20	4
Harry Bright	4	1
Dick Wilson	2	1
Con Corbeau	2	0 (played 15 games with Calumet)
Jack "Doc" Gibson	4	0
Harry Brown	5	0
"Tuff" Bellefeuille	2	0 (played 4 games with Calumet)
Cliff Hudson	1	0
Goalie: Darcy Regan	24 (3 shutouts) GAA 4.36	

**Portage Lake Hockey Team, 1906–07
International Hockey League Champion**
Clockwise from top left: *James Duggan (trainer), Darcy Regan (goal), John McNamara (manager), Barney Holden (point), Fred Lake (left wing), Bruce Stuart (center and captain), Jack Decarie (spare), Goldie Cochrane (rover), Grindy Forrester (right wing), Fred Taylor (cover point)*
(Michigan Technological University Archives and Copper Country Historical Collections)

The League Goes Out of Business

Discussion of the league's future occurred after every season but there was no indication that the league would not resume play for the 1907–08 season. During the summer and fall teams began planning for the coming season. A meeting was held in Chicago in late September 1907 to settle league membership questions, prepare a schedule, and give managers sufficient time to get players for the coming season. However, only three teams were represented—Calumet, Canadian Soo, and Michigan Soo. League officers were elected and plans were made for the season.

Elected Officers for 1907–8:
President: M.J. Kemp, Calumet
Vice President: W.L. Murdock, Michigan Soo
Secretary-Treasurer: M. Laughton, Canadian Soo

Following the meeting, Portage Lake's manager, John McNamara, claimed that he was not informed of the Chicago meeting and Pittsburgh officially notified the league that they would not compete in the 1907–08 season. There was talk that Pittsburgh was hoping to form a new league with Columbus, Cleveland, and Toronto. Another fall meeting was held in Marquette and President Kemp declared that at least four members would play in the coming season. The league approached Duluth on whether they would be interested in joining, but Duluth declined as they could not guarantee that they would have a satisfactory arena ready for the season. The league also talked about adding Kenora and a couple of teams from Manitoba, however a few weeks later, Michigan Soo announced that they were pulling out of the league citing a lack of players, and the league folded soon after.

During the three years of the IHL, hockey changed dramatically and professionalism became part of hockey in Canada. In November, the Ontario Professional Hockey League formed as the first avowedly professional hockey league in Canada, although hidden professionalism had been part of amateur hockey for several years. The Canadian players in the IHL now had the opportunity to return to Canada and openly accept payment for playing hockey. Other professional leagues formed and IHL players were sought by several teams in a bidding war for their services.

The league faced several challenges including a general economic downturn and sagging attendance in league cities. Teams could not generate enough revenue to offset the operating expenses and payrolls to compete with the salaries being offered by professional teams in Canada. Ultimately, the growth of professionalism in Canada would finish the IHL. The Western Pennsylvania Hockey League in Pittsburgh was re-established for the 1907–08 season and senior amateur hockey in the other four communities soon replaced the professional hockey teams of the IHL.

Although the IHL operated for only three seasons it attracted most of the top players of that era and played an integral part in changing the landscape for the acceptance of professional hockey in Canada.

IHL Career Goal Leaders

Lorne Campbell	(Pittsburgh, Portage Lake, Calumet)	108
Bill Taylor	(Canadian Soo, Michigan Soo)	99
Didier Pitre	(Michigan Soo)	77
Frank Schweitzer	(Michigan Soo)	70
Bruce Stuart	(Portage Lake)	68
Fred Lake	(Portage Lake)	66
Fred Strike	(Calumet)	56
Jack Ward	(Canadian Soo, Michigan Soo)	56
Ken Mallen	(Calumet)	55
Bert Morrison	(Portage Lake, Calumet)	38

IHL Games Played Leaders

Lorne Campbell	(Pittsburgh, Portage Lake, Calumet)	77
Billy Nicholson	(Calumet)	70
Joseph "Chief" Jones	(Michigan Soo)	69
Fred Lake	(Portage Lake)	67
Pud Hamilton	(Michigan Soo)	67
Bruce Stuart	(Portage Lake)	65
Barney Holden	(Portage Lake)	64
Jack Winchester	(Pittsburgh)	63
Fred Schweitzer	(Michigan Soo)	62
Bill Taylor	(Canadian Soo, Michigan Soo)	62
Jimmy Gardner	(Calumet, Pittsburgh)	62
Jack Ward	(Canadian Soo, Michigan Soo)	60
Jack Laviolette	(Michigan Soo)	60

Lorne Campbell, the IHL's all-time top goal scorer and games played leader. Campbell played three seasons for Pittsburgh but also played a few games for Portage Lake and Calumet at the end of the season.
(Michigan Technological University Archives and Copper Country Historical Collections)

CHAPTER 7
International Hockey League Players

COMPARED TO TODAY'S NATIONAL HOCKEY LEAGUE (NHL) players, IHL players were smaller—a typical player was about 5'7" to 5'8" and 150 pounds—but one has to remember that the average man was smaller during that era. For example, an average soldier was about 5'7" and 150 pounds. Fred Taylor was 5'9" and 165 pounds. Joe Hall was 5'10" and 175 pounds, similar to an average 20-year-old of today. Among the larger Portage Lake players were Jack Gibson at 6'0" and 185 pounds, Hod Stuart at 6'0" and 190 pounds, and Bruce Stuart at 6'2" and 180 pounds. The essential skills of skating, stick-handling, passing, shooting, and checking have not changed and the top players of that era excelled as they do in today's game. Hockey equipment was much different with little protection and players were expected to play the whole game as there were no substitutions. If a player was injured during a game and could not continue, there was a provision in the rules that the other team would drop one of their players. As a result, teams of that era had seven players and a few spares or substitutes would be used when another player could not start a game. The team captain typically assumed the role of coach.

Although the league operated for only three seasons with the five teams, ninety-seven men played in the league and virtually all of the players were from Canada. Thirty five players played ten games or less and several players played only one or two league games. When the IHL folded, most players returned to Canada and several went on to play on Stanley Cup winning teams. The players were among the best of that era and in fact, thirteen skaters and two goalies who played in the league have been inducted into the Hockey Hall of Fame in Toronto. Six played for the Portage Lake teams—Jack Gibson, Joe Hall, Riley Hern, Bruce Stuart, Hod Stuart, and Fred Taylor. Jack Gibson and Joe Linder have been honored with induction into the U.S. Hockey Hall of Fame in Eveleth, Minnesota. Every Stanley Cup winner from 1907 to 1916 had at least two players who had played in the IHL.

Outstanding Portage Lake Players and Hockey Hall of Famers

Joe Hall (1881–1919) played one season for the Portage Lake team (1905–06) and was among the league's top goal scorers with 33 goals in 20 games. He also led the league in penalties with 98 minutes and his aggressive play earned him the nickname "Bad." Another story on how he was given his nickname relates to a game played between Portage Lake and Calumet in the Palestra in December 1905. During the game, Hall was assessed a penalty by referee Doc Gibson and while serving the penalty, he used loud profane language in protest of the call. Over the next few days the incident grew in

Joe Hall

the local newspapers. One newspaper reported that he directed his comments to the Calumet fans and was escorted from the arena and placed under arrest. The local press called for a long suspension for his "bad" actions and that Hall must apologize to the citizens of Calumet before he would be allowed to play in the Palestra again. The league was prepared to punish and suspend Hall for his ungentlemanly actions, but following an apology to Calumet, he was not suspended and returned to play in Portage Lake's next game.

Another interesting story on Hall relates to his skates. Hall was born in England and moved to Canada at a young age and grew up in Brandon, Manitoba. He played hockey in Brandon and Winnipeg and in 1905 he complained to his neighbor that his hockey boots were uncomfortable and they would not last a season. His neighbor was George Tackaberry, a shoemaker who specialized in orthopedic shoes for the handicapped. After carefully measuring Hall's feet, he crafted a new durable and comfortable pair of boots. The word quickly spread and Tackaberry was flooded with orders from Hall's teammates and this style of boot became known as the Tackaberry. When George died in 1937, his wife sold the patent to the Canada Cycle and Motor Company (CCM) and the popular design became known as "CCM Tacks." When Joe Hall arrived in Houghton for the 1905–06 season he used a pair of Tackaberry skates.

After one season as a forward in Houghton, he returned to Canada and played for several teams as a defenseman. He was added to the roster of the Rat Portage (Kenora) Thistles for a Stanley Cup challenge against the Montreal Wanderers in January 1907, and although Hall did not play, the Thistles defeated the Wanderers and held the Cup for a couple of months until they were beaten in a rematch against the Wanderers. Hall was an important member of the Quebec Bulldogs in the National Hockey Association (NHA) when the team won the Stanley Cup in 1912 and 1913. The fans named him the Bulldogs' Most Popular Player following the 1913–14 season. While playing with the Bulldogs, he developed a nasty feud with the Montreal Canadiens star Newsy Lalonde and they would often fight during games between the two rival teams. When the National Hockey League (NHL) was formed in 1917, the Canadiens acquired Hall and the old adversaries become teammates, roomed together and became the best of friends.

In the spring of 1919, the NHL champion Canadiens headed to Seattle to take on the Pacific Coast Hockey League champion Metropolitans in a best-of-five Stanley Cup final. The series stood at two wins each and a tie when health officials cancelled the deciding game because of the influenza epidemic that had spread to many parts of North America. Hall and almost all of his teammates became ill during the series and many required hospitalization. Hall contracted pneumonia and died in the hospital, and the Stanley Cup final was cancelled. Hall was inducted into the Hockey Hall of Fame in 1961.

Riley Hern (1878–1929) was the goaltender for Portage Lake for three seasons including the first two seasons when they were an IHL team. Born in St. Mary's Ontario, he played hockey in St. Mary's

grandson, Allan Nicolls, played the role of captain of the Charlestown Chiefs in the famous 1977 hockey movie, Slap Shot.

Fred Lake (1883–1937) played a few games for the Portage Lake team in the 1902–03 season and then three seasons that Portage Lake was in the IHL. During each of the IHL seasons, Lake was one of the leading goal scorers for the team. When the IHL folded, Lake moved back to Canada and played for Winnipeg in the Manitoba Professional League and the Ottawa Hockey Club in the Eastern Canada Amateur Hockey Association (ECHA) and the National Hockey Association (NHA). He was a member of Ottawa Stanley Cup champion teams in 1909 and 1911.

Riley Hern

Fred lake

and Stratford before joining the Pittsburgh Keystones in the Western Pennsylvania Hockey League (WPHL) for two seasons and then moving to Houghton. He was a member of the 1903–04 Portage Lake team that won the U.S. Championship in 1904 and the IHL championship in 1906. Hern joined the Montreal Wanderers for the 1906–07 season and the team won the Stanley Cup four times and successfully defended the Cup in six out of seven challenges during his time with the Wanderers. The only challenge they lost was against the Rat Portage (Kenora) Thistles in January 1907, but the team reclaimed the Cup two months later. Hern retired from playing hockey in 1911 at the age of 30 and became a successful businessman in Montreal. He did, however, stay involved in the game as a representative for Spalding Sporting Goods, organized hockey leagues, and served as a NHL referee and goal judge. Hern has been regarded by some as being among the best goaltenders of all time and he was inducted into the Hockey Hall of Fame in 1963. An interesting note is that Hern's

Bert Morrison (1880–1969) played rover for the 1903–04 Portage Lake team and half of the following season when Portage Lake was an IHL member. In the 1903–04 season Morrison scored 94 goals in 25

Bert Morrison

Bruce Stuart

games for Portage Lake as the team won the U.S. Championship and the World's Championship. Morrison was born in Toronto, played at Upper Canada College, and for a Toronto amateur team before he joined the Pittsburgh Keystones for the 1901–02 season. While a member of the Toronto team he was investigated by the Ontario Hockey Association for accepting money to play hockey and he was always under suspicion after he joined the Keystones. He played for Calumet's IHL team in the 1906–07 season where he scored 28 goals in 22 games and then after the season he returned to Canada to play for the Montreal Shamrocks and the Toronto Pros in the Ontario Professional Hockey League (OPHL). In the 1907–08 season with Toronto, Morrison scored 22 goals in 10 games and led the team to the OPHL championship. He was injured in an exhibition game at the start of the following season and did not play again.

Bruce Stuart (1881–1961) was born in Ottawa and played several years for the Ottawa Hockey Club before joining the Pittsburgh Victorias for the 1902–03 season where he lead the team in scoring and was a league All-Star. After the Victorias were beaten by the Portage Lake team for the U.S. Championship, Stuart and his brother Hod Stuart were recruited to join the Portage Lake team for the following season. Bruce played four seasons in Houghton as a member of the 1903–04 Portage Lake team and three seasons in the IHL. He was one of the top goal scorers on the team; he scored 75 goals in 25 games during the 1903–04 championship team and 65 goals in 68 games in IHL play. Stuart is considered to be one of the best power forwards of the era as he combined rugged physical play with a scoring ability. He was over six feet tall and, in addition to scoring, he was among team leaders in penalty minutes.

When the IHL folded, Stuart joined the Montreal Wanderers for the 1907–08 and the team defeated Winnipeg to win the Stanley Cup in March 1908 and beat Toronto and Edmonton in other Cup challenges that year. Stuart then moved to Ottawa to captain the Senators to Stanley Cup wins in 1909, 1910, and 1911. Upset with a NHA proposal for a salary cap, he retired in 1911 and opened a shoe store in downtown Ottawa. Bruce was inducted into the Hockey Hall of Fame in 1961.

William "Hod" Stuart

William "Hod" Stuart (1879–1907) was one of hockey's best defensive players of his time. In an era when defensemen were expected to stay behind during the play, Stuart was known for his ability to score goals while playing a defensive role. Hod's early career began with the Rat Portage (Kenora) Thistles followed by two seasons with Ottawa and two seasons with Quebec City, before he joined the Pittsburgh Bankers for the 1902–03 season. He was named the best cover point in the league and was then recruited to join the Portage Lake team for the 1903–04 season. Hod scored 17 goals in 25 games as the team won the U.S. championship. With the formation of the IHL, Stuart left Portage Lake for the Calumet team where he became captain and manager of the team and manager of the new Palestra arena at a salary of $1,800 for the season. He led the Calumet team to the IHL championship and was named as the best cover point and one of the league's top players. He then joined the Pittsburgh team for the 1904–05 season and after Pittsburgh finished their season he was recruited back to Calumet for one game to help them beat Portage Lake. He started the next season with Pittsburgh, but voiced his unhappiness with some of the officiating and violence in the league and was released and joined the Montreal Wanderers of the Eastern Canada Amateur Hockey Association (ECAHA). It was about this time that teams in Canada began to realize that to retain the best players they needed to match the salaries of IHL players and Stuart was one of the players to benefit from the realization as Canadian leagues began to allow professional players on amateur teams. The Wanderers made Stuart the highest paid player of that era. He made an immediate impact and starred in a challenge series against Kenora in January 1907 although the Thistles won the Stanley Cup. The Wanderers went undefeated the rest of the season and defeated Kenora in March 1907 in a rematch to claim the Stanley Cup. Tragically it would be Stuart's only Stanley Cup.

After the hockey season, Stuart returned to Ottawa to work for his father's construction company. He was assigned to a building project in Belleville, Ontario but during a Sunday break from work, Stuart suffered a fatal injury when he struck his head on rocks while diving into unfamiliar waters at the Bay of Quinte. In the fall, the ECAHA decided to host an all-star game, the first of its kind to be played in any sport, to raise money for Stuart's widow and children. The Hod Stuart Memorial Game was held on January 2, 1908 and featured the Montreal Wanderers playing a team of the top players from other teams in the ECAHA. Hod Stuart was selected as one of the original inductees when the Hockey Hall of Fame was created in 1945.

Fred Taylor

Fred Taylor (1885–1979) was hockey's first superstar and was the cover point on the Portage Lake team that won the 1906 and 1907 IHL championships. Taylor was born in Tara, Ontario and grew up in Listowel where he played hockey as a teenager. In 1904, following an outstanding season with the Listowel Mintos, he was approached by the Ontario Hockey Association to sign with a Toronto team for the following season but he refused and was recruited to join a team in Thessalon, Ontario. Shortly after arriving in Thessalon, he received a letter from the OHA that he was banned from playing for an Ontario team. Taylor appealed the decision and it was denied but he stayed in Thessalon during the winter, worked in a local hotel, and practiced with the team. In the fall of 1905, Taylor joined the Portage la Prairie, Manitoba team and played a few games before several IHL teams approached him to join their team. The Dawson City team also contacted Taylor to see if he would be interested in joining them as they traveled across Canada for their Stanley Cup challenge series against the Ottawa Silver Seven.

In February 1906, he joined the Portage Lake team and scored 11 goals in 6 games and helped the team win the IHL championship. Grindy Forrester was a member of the Portage Lake team and former captain of the Thessalon team and played an important role in convincing Taylor to come to Houghton. Taylor returned for the 1906–07 season and the team repeated as IHL champion. When the IHL folded, Taylor joined the Ottawa Hockey Club ("Silver Seven") of the Eastern Canada Amateur Hockey Association where he played for two seasons for an annual salary and promise of a civil service job. It is while playing for Ottawa that he was given the nickname "Cyclone." After witnessing an outstanding game by Taylor, Malcolm Bryce, an Ottawa newspaper reporter, wrote "I understand that he was 'Tornado' when he played in Manitoba, and 'Whirlwind' when he played in the IHL, but starting today, I am calling him 'Cyclone' Taylor." The team won the Stanley Cup in his second season, but the Renfrew Creamery Kings of the new National Hockey Association signed him for a reported $5,250 for 12 games the 1909–10 season and this made him the highest paid Canadian athlete. Renfrew also signed Lester Patrick, Frank Patrick, and Newsy Lalonde to contracts with high salaries so the fans often referred to the team as the Renfrew Millionaires. The Renfrew team folded after the 1911 season and Taylor became property of the NHA's Montreal Wanderers in a dispersal draft but he couldn't reach an agreement to play for the team and so he sat out the season. Meanwhile, Lester and Frank Patrick formed the Pacific Coast Hockey Association (PCHA) and persuaded Taylor to move west where he joined the Vancouver Millionaires for the 1912–13 season. Taylor was moved to a forward position and helped lead the Millionaires to their only Stanley Cup in 1915. He won five scoring titles while playing for the Millionaires and retired in 1921.

Taylor was elected as a charter member of the Hockey Hall of Fame in 1945 and in 1950 he was named as Canada's top hockey player of the first half of the twentieth century. In 1957, his oldest son, Fred Taylor, Jr., started a chain of popular hockey equipment stores in the Vancouver area called Cyclone Taylor Sports and it still operates today. Taylor died in 1979 at the age of 95.

Jack "Doc" Gibson

and Dee promoted the idea of a professional hockey league, and play began in the International Hockey League in December 1904. The five team league lasted for three seasons as hockey's first professional league. Gibson played for Portage Lake in the first season, was a referee in the second season, and played two games for Portage Lake in the third season. When the IHL folded, Gibson closed his Houghton office and moved his dental practice to Calgary, Alberta. He was inducted as an administrator into the United States Hockey Hall of Fame in 1973 and as a builder into the Hockey Hall of Fame in Toronto in 1976.

Joe Linder

Jack "Doc" Gibson (1879–1954) was born in Berlin, Ontario and played for Waterloo/Berlin and Berlin hockey teams before attending the Detroit College of Medicine to study dentistry. For three seasons he played for the Detroit College of Medicine and Berlin hockey teams. In 1900 he moved to Houghton, Michigan to set up a dental practice. In his first winter he joined a Portage Lake amateur hockey team and they won the Upper Peninsula championship. Within a couple seasons, Portage Lake was one of the top teams in the United States and Houghton had one of the finest ice arenas in the country. In the fall of 1903, Gibson and James Dee, a local entrepreneur, made the decision to recruit the best players from Canada and pay them to play hockey. The 1903–04 Portage Lake team was an outstanding team that defeated the Pittsburgh Victorias for the United States championship and they defeated the Montreal Wanderers in a challenge series for what was billed as the World's Championship. In the summer and fall of 1904 Gibson

Joe Linder (1884–1948) was born in Hancock, Michigan and starred in baseball, football, and hockey at Hancock Central High School. When he was a high school sophomore, Doc Gibson recruited Linder as a substitute defenseman for three games with the 1903–04 Portage Lake team. In the 1905–06 season, Linder was coach of the

Hancock high school team and dressed for one game as a substitute for the IHL's Calumet team. He graduated from high school in 1906 and played on local amateur teams for several years. Then in 1912 he moved to Duluth, Minnesota where he worked in a factory and played three seasons for the Duluth Curling Club hockey team. In 1915 he was laid off and returned to the Copper Country where he was employed as a machinist for the Calumet and Hecla Mining Company in Calumet. In 1920 he moved to Superior, Wisconsin to open a general store with his brother-in-law and became active in the local business and sports community. Many have described Linder as "the first great American born hockey player." He was inducted into the United States Hockey Hall of Fame in 1975.

Other International Hockey League Stars and Hockey Hall of Famers

Lorne Campbell (1879–1957) was born in Montreal and played for the Montreal Hockey Club before he was recruited for the Pittsburgh Bankers in the Western Pennsylvania Hockey League (WPHL). He played three seasons for the Bankers and when the IHL formed he joined the Pittsburgh Pros, a team of the best players from the WPHL. Campbell played three seasons for the Pittsburgh Pros and was among the top players in the league and IHL career leader in games played (77) and goals scored (108). In the first two IHL seasons, Pittsburgh ended its season before other teams in the league, so Campbell signed as a free agent with Portage Lake for four games to help catch the Calumet team for the 1905 league championship. Although he scored six goals in the four games, Calumet won the championship. In the second season, Campbell signed with Calumet at the end of the season for one game to beat Portage Lake. After the IHL folded, Campbell played one season with the Winnipeg Maple Leafs in which they were unsuccessful in a Stanley Cup challenge against the Montreal Wanderers. The following season he returned to Pittsburgh to play for the Pittsburgh Athletic Club in the WPHL and then retired in 1910 after he played a few games with Cobalt in the National Hockey Association (NHA).

Jimmy Gardner (1881–1940) was born in Montreal and played four seasons for the Montreal AAA Hockey Club and one season with the Montreal Wanderers of the Federal Hockey League before he was recruited by Calumet in the IHL. While he was a member of the Montreal AAA team they won the Stanley Cup in 1902 and 1903, and when he played for the Wanderers, the team challenged Portage Lake in March 1904 for what was billed as the World's Championship; Portage Lake was victorious in the two-game series. Gardner played two seasons with Calumet and one season with Pittsburgh in the IHL and was a member of the 1905 Calumet championship team. He returned to Montreal and played one season with the Montreal Shamrocks and then in 1908 became player/manager for the Montreal Wanderers for three seasons in which the team won the Stanley Cup twice—1909 and 1910. In 1911, Gardner was recruited by the New Westminister Royals in the new Pacific Coast Hockey League (PCHL) where he played two seasons before returning to Montreal as coach/captain for the Canadiens for two seasons before retiring in 1915. He stayed in the game as an on-ice official and coached several teams including the NHL's Hamilton Tigers during the 1924–25 season. The Tigers finished in first place but the team went on strike over a salary dispute before the final playoff series with the Montreal Canadiens. The NHL President Frank Calder disqualified the team and awarded the title to the Canadiens. The Canadiens proved no match for the Victoria Cougars, winners of the Western Canada Hockey League, and the Cougars became the last non-NHL team to win the Stanley Cup. In the summer of 1925, the Hamilton Tigers were sold and became the New York Americans, but Gardner did not move with the team. He later coached in Providence, Sherbrooke, and Verdun. Gardner died in 1940 and was inducted into the Hockey Hall of Fame in 1962.

Joseph "Chief" Jones (1879–1959) was the goaltender on the 1902–03 Portage Lake team that won the U.S. Championship. He was born in Renfrew, Ontario and ended up in Minnesota playing for the St. Paul Victorias. In January 1902, the Victorias traveled to Houghton to play the Portage Lake team and although the Victorias were soundly defeated, Jack Gibson was impressed with Jones' play and recruited him for the 1902–03 team. Jones played one season with Portage Lake and then moved to Sault Ste. Marie, Michigan where he played four seasons for the Michigan Soo team, three while the team played in the IHL. He was one of the top goaltenders in the league. His nickname, "Chief," came from his Native American heritage. In 1909 Jones signed with the Cobalt Silver Chiefs of the National Hockey Association (NHA) where he played two years before joining the Waterloo Colts in the Ontario Professional Hockey League (OPHL) for a season before he retired in 1911.

Edouard "Newsy" Lalonde (1887–1970) was born in Cornwall, Ontario and earned his nickname "Newsy" by working in a local newsprint plant as a youth. Lalonde started his hockey career in Cornwall and played one season in Woodstock before he was recruited to join the Canadian Soo team in the IHL for 1906–07 season where he became one of the top players in the league. In 1907, he signed with the Toronto Professionals in the Ontario Professional Hockey league and played for two seasons before he joined the newly formed Montreal Canadiens of the NHA for the 1909–1910 season where he scored 16 goals in six games. He scored the first-ever goal for the Canadiens. After six games, team owner J. Ambrose O'Brien traded him to the Renfew Creamery Kings for the balance of the season. Lalonde continued his scoring exploits and scored 22 goals in five games, including nine goals in a game in March 1910, and won the NHA's first scoring title. The following season, he returned to Montreal but signed with the Vancouver Millionaires of the PCHL for the 1911–12 season where he scored 27 goals in 15 games and won the PCHA scoring title. Wanting to regain his scoring, the Canadiens purchased Lalonde's rights and he returned to the Canadiens for the 1912–13 season for $2,300. Lalonde remained with the team for ten seasons and was the team captain/coach when the Canadiens defeated the Portland Rosebuds for their first Stanley Cup in 1916. When the NHL was formed in November 1917, Lalonde played on a line with Joe Malone and Didier Pitre in the first NHL game on December 19, 1917 but missed part of the season due to injuries. In the following season, Lalonde won his first NHL scoring title and the Canadiens played Seattle in the Stanley Cup series, but after five games in which each team won two games and one was tied, the deciding game was cancelled because of the influenza epidemic. In 1922, Lalonde was traded to Saskatoon of the PCHL where he received $5,000 for the season and won the league's scoring title. In 1926, he was traded to the New York Americans and was named player coach but only played one game and spent the rest of the season as coach/manager. He then served as head coach for the Ottawa Senators and the Montreal Canadiens before retiring from hockey in 1935. During his career Lalonde was the scoring champion five times in the three leagues and when he retired he held the record for the most goals scored by a professional hockey player of 543 goals. The record was not broken until Maurice Richard scored 544 goals in his career. Although Lalonde was a top goal scorer, he was one of the meanest players of his era, hated by opposition players and even some of his teammates.

Lalonde is best remembered as a hockey player, but he was just as prominent in lacrosse. He was an outstanding player on lacrosse teams in Montreal and Vancouver that won national championships, and in 1950 Lalonde was named greatest lacrosse player of the first-half of the century. He was inducted into the Hockey Hall of Fame in 1950 and the Canadian Lacrosse Hall of Fame in 1965.

Jack Laviotte (1879–1960) was born in Belleville, Ontario but grew up in Valleyfield, Quebec where he learned to play hockey and lacrosse. He began his organized hockey career playing for teams in Montreal, and then in 1904 he was signed as a defenseman by Michigan Soo in the new IHL. Laviotte was an all-star in his three seasons with Michigan Soo and when the IHL folded he returned to Montreal to play for the Montreal Shamrocks of the Eastern Canadian Amateur Hockey Association (ECAHA) for two seasons. With the formation of the National Hockey Association (NHA) in December 1909, team/league owner Ambrose O'Brien asked Laviotte to put together a team in Montreal of French Canadian players to play as the "Les Canadiens." Among those that he would sign were Newsy Lalonde, Didier Pitre, and George Vezina. Laviotte was the first player, coach, and manager of the Montreal Canadiens and the team that he built would go on to be the most successful franchise in professional hockey. Laviotte was star player for nine seasons with the Canadiens and was a member of the team that defeated the Portland Rosebuds for the Stanley Cup in 1916. He was also a race car driver and his hockey career ended in 1918 when he lost his foot in a car crash. Laviotte was inducted into the Hockey Hall of Fame in 1962.

Hugh Lehman (1885–1961) was the goaltender for the Canadian Soo team in the IHL for the 1906–07 season. Lehman was born in Pembroke, Ontario and played for the Pembroke Lumber Kings before signing with the Canadian Soo team. He signed with the Michigan Soo team for the 1907–08 season, but they folded before any games were played. He returned to Pembroke for a season and then joined the Berlin team in the Ontario Professional Hockey League (OPHL) where he played for three seasons. Nicknamed "Old Eagle Eyes," Lehman was among the first goaltenders to wander from his net and folklore has it that he scored a goal while playing for Berlin. He was also the first goaltender to pass the puck to his defensemen and forwards. In 1911, Lehman headed west and played three seasons for New Westminister Royals and eight seasons for Vancouver Millionaires in the Pacific Coast Hockey League (PCHA) and four seasons with the Vancouver Maroons in the Western Canada Hockey League (WHL). He is the PCHA all-time leader in games played, wins, and shutouts, and while a member of the Millionaires he appeared in six Stanley Cup finals, winning only once in 1915. In 1926, he joined the Chicago Blackhawks of the NHL where he played one season as goaltender and split the second as goaltender and coach. Lehman retired in 1928 as one hockey's top goaltenders and then worked in road construction, eventually owning a paving company. Lehman was inducted into the Hockey Hall of Fame in 1958.

Ken Mallen (1884–1930) was born in Morrisburg, Ontario and played with Cornwall and the Montreal Wanderers in the Federal Amateur Hockey League before he was signed by the Calumet team for the 1904–05 season. Mallen played for the Wanderers when they challenged Portage Lake for the World's Championship in 1904. In his first season with Calumet, he established his reputation as a goal scorer with 38 goals in 24 games and helped lead the team to the IHL championship. He returned to Calumet for the second and third season but was bothered by rough play in the league so he did not play all of the games. In subsequent years, Mallen played for several teams including the Toronto Pros, Pittsburgh Athletic Club, Ottawa Senators, and Quebec Bulldogs before he moved out west to play in the Pacific Coast Hockey League (PCHA). There he played three seasons for the New Westminister Royals, one with the Vancouver Millionaires, one with the Victoria Aristocrats, and one with the Spokane Canaries before retiring in 1917. Mallen was a member of the Millionaires when they defeated the Ottawa Senators in a three-game series in 1915 to win the Stanley Cup. Teammate Cyclone Taylor was the leading scorer for the Millionaires. After Mallen retired, he worked as a referee and a skating instructor in Ottawa and London, Ontario.

His older brother, Jim (1881–1954), also played for Calumet in the 1905–06 and 1906–07 seasons but was limited in the number of games due to a knee injury. Jim played for several other professional teams and coached at Princeton and St. Lawrence University. He also coached the 1932 U.S. Olympic hockey team.

Didier Pitre (1883–1934) was one of the fastest skaters of the era and was nicknamed "Cannonball" for his wrist shot. He was born in Valleyfield, Quebec and played in Montreal before signing as a free agent forward by Michigan Soo in the new IHL. He played three seasons for Michigan Soo and led the league in goal scoring in the 1905–06 season with 41 goals in 22 games. He was a league all-star and was among the top goal scorers in his IHL career. When the IHL folded in 1907, Pitre was signed by the Montreal Shamrocks for the 1907–08 season. He joined Edmonton for the start of the following season, but after three games he signed with the Renfrew Creamery Kings. It was not unusual that players of this era would switch teams annually or even during the season for better contracts. In 1909, Pitre became the first player signed by Jack Laviotte for the Montreal Canadiens in the new NHA where he would play for 13 seasons. In 1913, the Canadiens asked him to take a pay cut from $3,000 to $800 for season but he refused and signed with the Vancouver Millionaires of the PCHL for the 1913–14 season. However, after the one season with Vancouver, Pitre returned to the Canadiens and helped lead them to their first Stanley Cup in 1916. He retired in 1923 and returned to Sault Ste. Marie, Michigan where he refereed and coached local teams. Pitre was inducted into the Hockey Hall of Fame in 1962.

Art Sixsmith (1882–1969) was born in Ottawa, Ontario and played for several Ottawa teams prior to moving to Pittsburgh. In 1901, Sixsmith met Arthur McSwigan and the two men founded the Western Pennsylvania Hockey League (WPHL) and convinced several of the top players from Canada to play in this new league with the promise of good jobs and a small stipend to play hockey. Sixsmith was manager and captain of the Pittsburgh Keystones for one season and the Pittsburgh Victorias for two seasons before the WPHL teams were consolidated into the Pittsburgh Professionals for IHL. Sixsmith was captain, rover, and one of top goal scorers for the Pros for two seasons. In 1906 he signed with Portage la Prairie in the Manitoba Professional Hockey League (MPHL) and then in 1907 he returned to Pittsburgh to play for the Pittsburgh Bankers when the WPHL was revived after the IHL folded. Sixsmith retired after two seasons with the Bankers and went into the banking business working his way up to become Andrew Mellon's personal assistant. Mellon took over his father's bank and founded Alcoa, Gulf Oil, Union Steel, and numerous other companies and by the early 1920s he was one of the richest men in the United States. In 1921, Mellon was appointed as the Secretary of the Treasury by President Harding and would remain in that position under Presidents Coolidge and Hoover. Sixsmith continued to serve as Mellon's assistant during Mellon's tenure as U.S. Treasury Secretary.

His younger brother, Garnet (1887–1967), played three seasons for the Pittsburgh Victorias in the WPHL. The team won the league championship in 1904 but they were defeated by Portage Lake for the U.S. championship. Garnet played a couple of games with the Pittsburgh Pros in the first IHL season but was released and then signed with the Canadian Soo team. He rejoined the Pros for the 1905–06 season, but an ankle injury shorten his season. Garnet finished his career with Pittsburgh teams in the WPHL after the IHL folded and he retired in 1909.

Tommy Smith (1885–1966) was born in Ottawa, Ontario, played for several Ottawa teams, and was a member of the Ottawa Silver Seven when they won the Stanley Cup in 1906. He was signed by the Pittsburgh Pros for the 1906–07 team and scored 31 goals in 23 games to be one of the top goal scorers in the league. When the IHL folded, he stayed in Pittsburgh and played for the Lyceums for one season and part of the next before signing with the Brantford team in the Ontario Professional Hockey League (OPHL) for the rest of the 1908–09 season. He missed most of the 1909–10 season with typhoid fever and then played for several teams including Galt, Moncton, Toronto Shamrocks, Quebec Bulldogs, and the Montreal Canadiens. While playing center for four seasons with the Bulldogs, he lead the NHA in goal scoring two seasons and the team won the Stanley Cup in 1913. Smith was also a member with the Montreal Canadiens when they were defeated by the Seattle Metropolitans in the 1917 Stanley Cup finals. He was inducted into the Hockey Hall of Fame in 1973.

Fred Strike (1880–1967) was born in Montreal and played hockey for the Montreal AAA and Montreal Wanderers before he was signed by the Calumet team in the IHL for the 1904–05 season. Strike was the team's top goal scorer with 44 goals in 24 games and helped lead the team to the league championship. He was also the league's top goal scorer and a league all-star. Strike played a second season with Calumet, but then returned to Canada to play a few games for Ottawa in the Federal Amateur Hockey League and Toronto in the National Hockey Association in 1912–13.

Billy "Lady" Taylor (1880–1942) was born in Paris, Ontario and played in Paris and Brantford before signing with the Canadian Soo team in the new IHL. He played three seasons with the Canadian Soo team and part of the 1905–06 season with the Michigan Soo team when the Canadian Soo team folded during the season. He was an all-star rover and second to only Lorne Campbell as the top goal scorer in his IHL career with 99 goals in 62 games. When the IHL folded, Taylor signed to play with Brantford in the Ontario Professional Hockey League (OPHL) for the 1907–08 season and he was second in goal scoring to Newsy Lalonde. The following season he played for several teams in a troubling year in which he was charged and fined after threating to kill his estranged wife and was released by the Berlin OPHL team for breaking training rules. In 1912, Taylor had an unsuccessful tryout with the Toronto Tecumsehs in the NHA and entered the Canadian Army during World War I but was wounded while serving overseas and never played hockey again.

Edwin Chaucer Elliott (1879–1913) was born in Kingston, Ontario and played hockey and football at Queen's University in Kingston. He left university before graduating to organize a semi-professional baseball league with teams from Ontario and New York and in addition to playing baseball he coached several Canadian football teams. In 1903 he began a career as a hockey referee with the Ontario Hockey Association and refereed 27 games in the IHL in the 1905–06 season in response to complaints about the referees during first season of the league. Elliott was regarded as one of the best referees in Canada and was always in high demand. He died of cancer at the age of 34 and was inducted into the Hockey Hall of Fame in 1961.

George McNamara (1886–1952) was born in Penetanguishene, Ontario but the family moved to Sault Ste. Marie, Ontario when he was a young boy. McNamara played on a local hockey team and was recruited by the IHL's Canadian Soo team where he played three games as a defenseman during the 1906–07 season. After the IHL folded, McNamara played for several professional teams including the Montreal Shamrocks, Waterloo Colts, Halifax Crescents, Toronto Tecumsehs, and Toronto Blueshirts. He was a valued member of the Toronto Blueshirts when they won the Stanley Cup in 1914. In 1916 he joined the Canadian Army and was a member of the Toronto 228th Battalion team that participated in the NHA before the team had to drop out of the league when they were ordered to active duty overseas in February 1917. After the war, McNamara returned to the Sault and coached the Soo Greyhounds for six seasons. In 1924 the team won the Allan Cup in recognition as Canada's best amateur team. George and a younger brother, Howard (1890–1940), founded the McNamara Construction Company and developed it into a prosperous firm in Ontario. George McNamara was inducted into the Hockey Hall of Fame in 1958.

Although Howard was too young to play in the IHL he played defense with his brother on the Halifax Crescents where they were known as the "Dynamite Twins." Howard was captain of the Montreal Canadiens in 1916 when the team won its first Stanley Cup, and he played with his brother on the Toronto 228th Battalion team.

A third brother, Harold (1889–1937), played a few games for both the Canadian Soo and Michigan Soo IHL teams, and then played on several other professional teams including the Halifax Crescents, Cobalt Silver Kings, Waterloo Colts, Renfrew Creamery Kings, and Montreal Canadiens.

Oliver Seibert (1881–1944) first played hockey in his hometown of Berlin, Ontario and was a teammate of Jack Gibson on the 1900 Berlin OHA senior championship team and the Berlin team that played an exhibition series in St. Louis, Missouri in 1901. Seibert was a versatile player and is believed to be one of the first to use a wrist shot. He played on several championship teams in Berlin before he signed as a free agent with the IHL's Canadian Soo team on January 31, 1905 for $30 per week and board. However, in his first game against Calumet on February 2, he suffered a season-ending broken leg that ended his IHL career. Seibert later played for Berlin, London, and Guelph in the Ontario Professional Hockey League (OPHL) and was inducted into the Hockey Hall of Fame in 1961. His son, Earl Seibert, played in the NHL with the New York Rangers, Detroit, and Chicago in a seventeen year career and is also an honored member in the Hockey Hall of Fame.

Marty Walsh (1884–1915) was born in Kingston, Ontario and played junior hockey in Kingston and at Queen's University before signing as a free agent with the Canadian Soo team in the IHL for the 1906-07 season. Unfortunately due to an injury he played only seven games with the Canadian Soo team. He joined the Ottawa Senators in 1907 and played five seasons and was a member of the team as they won the Stanley Cup in 1909, 1910, and 1911. In 1911, he scored ten goals in Stanley Cup challenge game against Port Arthur, and then after the season when Bruce Stuart retired, Walsh was named team captain. He played one more season with Ottawa and then headed west to start a cattle ranch. He later coached the Edmonton Eskimos for one season but fell ill to tuberculosis and died in 1915. Many believe that Walsh was one of the best hockey players that Kingston ever produced. He was inducted into the Hockey Hall of Fame in 1962.

A List of All IHL Players

The names, place of birth, and teams of all of the players that played in the International Hockey League are shown below. However, there are a few players for whom their first name or place of birth is not known. The players who have been inducted into the Hockey Hall of Fame, in Toronto, Ontario are identified in bold.

PLAYER	PLACE OF BIRTH	IHL TEAMS	GAMES	GOALS
Billy Baird	Ottawa, Ontario	(1904–05) Pittsburgh	9	1
		(1905–06) Pittsburgh	24	4
		(1906–07) Pittsburgh	11	0
Tuff Bellefeuille	Petawawa, Ontario	(1906–07) Portage Lake	2	0
		(1906–07) Calumet	4	2
William Bellefeuille	Petawawa, Ontario	(1905–06) Calumet	12	1
		(1906–07) Calumet	21	12
Haddo Black	Windsor, Ontario	(1904–05) Pittsburgh	17	7
		(1905–06) Canadian Soo	2	1
Harry Bright	Montreal, Quebec	(1904–05) Portage Lake	8	9
		(1905–06) Portage Lake	9	7
		(1906–07) Portage Lake	4	1
		(1906–07) Pittsburgh	7	0
Harry Brown	Belleville, Ontario	(1906–07) Portage Lake	5	0
Roy Brown	Mitchell, Ontario	(1904–05) Canadian Soo	24	9
		(1906–07) Canadian Soo	22	7
Lorne Campbell	Montreal, Quebec	(1904–05) Pittsburgh	24	29
		(1904–05) Portage Lake	4	6
		(1905–06) Pittsburgh	24	35
		(1905–06) Calumet	1	3
		(1906–07) Pittsburgh	24	35
Pete Charlton	New Ferry, UK Hometown: Berlin, Ontario	(1906–07) Michigan Soo	9	2

PLAYER	PLACE OF BIRTH	IHL TEAMS	GAMES	GOALS
Frank Clifton	Alliston, Ontario	(1904–05) Canadian Soo	13	8
		(1905–06) Canadian Soo	15	20
		(1906–07) Michigan Soo	4	0
Goldie Cochrane	Berlin`, Ontario	(1906–07) Portage Lake	17	15
Charles Collins	Collingwood, Ontario	(1904–05) Canadian Soo	22	22
Con Corbeau	Penetanguishene, Ontario	(1905–06) Pittsburgh	3	1
		(1905–06) Canadian Soo	9	0
		(1905–06) Calumet	7	0
		(1906–07) Portage Lake	2	0
		(1906–07) Calumet	15	4
Charles "Shorty" Corbett	Omemee, Ontario	(1904–05) Canadian Soo	1	0
Ed Decarie	Hawkesbury, Ontario	(1905–06) Calumet	10	6
		(1905–06) Canadian Soo	4	5
		(1906–07) Calumet	18	10
Ambrose Degray	Cornwall, Ontario	(1906–07) Canadian Soo	2	1
Ted Drolet	unknown	(1906–07) Canadian So	1	0
Billy "Peg" Duval	Ottawa, Ontario	(1904–05) Pittsburgh	13	4
Charles "Lal" Earls	Toronto, Ontario	(1904–05) Calumet	9	0
Alex Findlay	Sault Ste. Marie, Ontario	(1904–05) Canadian Soo	1	1
Walter Forrest	Waterloo, Ontario	(1905–06) Portage Lake	5	0
Grindy Forrester	Barrie, Ontario	(1905–06) Portage Lake	20	4
		(1906–07) Portage Lake	22	15
Jimmy Gardner	Montreal, Quebec	(1904–05) Calumet	23	16
		(1905–06) Calumet	19	3
		(1906–07) Pittsburgh	20	10

PLAYER	PLACE OF BIRTH	IHL TEAMS	GAMES	GOALS
Horace Gaul	Gaspe, Quebec	(1906–07) Pittsburgh	18	10
Jack "Doc" Gibson	Berlin, Ontario	(1904–05) Portage Lake (1906–07) Portage Lake	24 4	2 0
Edward "Texas" Gillard	Paris, Ontario	(1904–05) Canadian Soo	18 1	2 goalie
Joe "Bad" Hall	Staffordshire, UK Hometown: Brandon, MB	(1905–06) Portage Lake	20	33
Andy Haller	Hancock, Michigan	(1904–05) Portage Lake	1	0
Billy "Pud" Hamilton	Kingston, Ontario	(1904–05) Michigan Soo (1905–06) Michigan Soo (1906–07) Michigan Soo	24 20 23	5 7 4
Riley Hern	St. Mary's, Ontario	(1904–05) Portage Lake (1905–06) Portage Lake	24 20	goalie goalie
Ed Hogan	Quebec City, Quebec	(1906–07) Pittsburgh	17	5
Barney Holden	Winnipeg, Manitoba	(1904–05) Portage Lake (1905–06) Portage Lake (1906–07) Portage Lake	24 20 20	9 9 4
Cliff Hollingsworth	Prescott, Ontario	(1905–06) Canadian Soo	2	0
Eddie "Ted" Howell	Guelph, Ontario	(1904–05) Michigan Soo (1905–06) Michigan Soo	24 22	7 3
Cliff "Dick" Hudson	Brockville, Ontario	(1906–07) Portage Lake	1	0
Joseph "Chief" Jones	Renfrew, Ontario	(1904–05) Michigan Soo (1905–06) Michigan Soo (1906–07) Michigan Soo	24 22 23	goalie goalie goalie

PLAYER	PLACE OF BIRTH	IHL TEAMS	GAMES	GOALS
Alwyn Kent	Ottawa, Ontario	(1904–05) Pittsburgh	12	3
		(1905–06) Pittsburgh	13	9
Fred Lake	Moosomin, Saskatchewan	(1904–05) Portage Lake	24	14
		(1905–06) Portage Lake	20	25
		(1906–07) Portage Lake	23	27
Edouard "Newsy" Lalonde	Cornwall, Ontario	(1906–07) Canadian Soo	18	29
Bert Larson	Houghton, Michigan	(1905–06) Calumet	1	0
Jack Laviolette	Belleville, Ontario	(1904–05) Michigan Soo	24	15
		(1905–06) Michigan Soo	17	15
		(1906–07) Michigan Soo	19	10
Hugh Lehman	Pembroke, Ontario	(1906–07) Canadian Soo	24	goalie
Charlie "Chas" Liffiton	Montreal, Quebec	(1904–05) Portage Lake	14	6
Ernie Liffiton	Montreal, Quebec	(1906–07) Pittsburgh	13	1
Joe Linder	Hancock, Michigan	(1905–06) Calumet	1	0
Jim Mallen	Morrisburg, Ontario	(1905–06) Calumet	4	3
		(1906–07) Calumet	1	0
Ken Mallen	Morrisburg, Ontario	(1904–05) Calumet	24	38
		(1905–06) Calumet	5	4
		(1906–07) Calumet	11	13
Jack MacKay	Scotland Hometown: Ottawa, Ontario	(1904–05) Pittsburgh	9	goalie
Pete Maltman	Oshawa, Ontario	(1904–05) Canadian Soo	24	goalie
Jack Marks	Belleville, Ontario	(1906–07) Canadian Soo	14	13
--- McCabe	unknown	(1904–05) Calumet	3	0

PLAYER	PLACE OF BIRTH	IHL TEAMS	GAMES	GOALS
George McCarron	Quebec City, Quebec	(1904–05) Pittsburgh	4	0
		(1904–05) Michigan Soo	1	0
Alfred "Cap" McDonald	Mattawa, Ontario	(1905–06) Michigan Soo	9	6
		(1905–06) Calumet	8	4
		(1906–07) Calumet	24	5
Charles McLurg	Woodstock, Ontario	(1904–05) Canadian Soo	2	0
Jack McMaster	Winnipeg, Manitoba	(1904–05) Portage Lake	1	2
		(1904–05) Pittsburgh	4	3
Reddy McMillan	Cornwall, Ontario	(1904–05) Calumet	22	5
		(1905–06) Michigan Soo	19	22
George McNamara	Penetanguishene, Ontario	(1906–07) Canadian Soo	3	0
Harold McNamara	Randolph, Ontario	(1905–06) Canadian Soo	2	1
		(1906–07) Canadian Soo	2	0
		(1906–07) Michigan Soo	4	0
Harry McRobie	Iroquois, Ontario	(1906–07) Canadian Soo	24	5
Tom "Rube" Melville	Montreal, Quebec	(1904–05) Pittsburgh	7	4
		(1905–06) Pittsburgh	2	0
Milford Milne	Chelsea, Quebec	(1905–06) Canadian Soo	4	0
		(1905–06) Calumet	1	0
Bert Morrison	Toronto, Ontario	(1904–05) Portage Lake	12	10
		(1906–07) Calumet	22	28
Billy Nicholson	Montreal, Quebec	(1904–05) Calumet	24	goalie
		(1905–06) Calumet	21	goalie
		(1906–07) Calumet	25	goalie

PLAYER	PLACE OF BIRTH	IHL TEAMS	GAMES	GOALS
Dick O'Leary	Prescott, Ontario	(1904–05) Canadian Soo (1904–05) Pittsburgh	13 2	2 0
Joseph Ouelette	Ottawa, Ontario	(1906–07) Canadian Soo	1	0
Didier Pitre	Valleyfield, Quebec	(1904–05) Michigan Soo (1905–06) Michigan Soo (1906–07) Michigan Soo	13 22 23	11 41 25
--- Powell	unknown	(1904–05) Canadian Soo	1	0
Antoine Ratte	Kingsey, Quebec	(1905–06) Canadian Soo	15	3
Darcy Regan	Orillia, Ontario	(1905–06) Canadian Soo (1906–07) Portage Lake	15 24	goalie goalie
Ed "Muggins" Roberts	Ottawa, Ontario	(1904–05) Pittsburgh (1905–06) Pittsburgh	24 24	10 19
William "Jigger" Robinson	Kingston, Ontario	(1904–05) Michigan Soo (1905–06) Pittsburgh	16 4	9 2
Charlie Ross	Ottawa, Ontario	(1906–07) Pittsburgh	7	0
Edward "Dutch" Schaefer	Tavistock, Ontario	(1906–07) Canadian Soo	21	5
Frank Schweitzer	Stratford, Ontario	(1904–05) Michigan Soo (1905–06) Michigan Soo (1906–07) Michigan Soo	18 22 22	18 25 27
Bob "Doctor" Scott	Pembroke, Ontario	(1904–05) Calumet (1905–06) Calumet (1906–07) Calumet	14 20 19	6 10 14
Oliver Seibert	Berlin, Ontario	(1904–05) Canadian Soo	1	0

PLAYER	PLACE OF BIRTH	IHL TEAMS	GAMES	GOALS
William "Cooney" Shields	Guelph, Ontario	(1904–05) Calumet	7	4
		(1904–05) Portage Lake	10	7
		(1905–06) Calumet	21	2
		(1906–07) Calumet	17	6
Art Sixsmith	Ottawa, Ontario	(1904–05) Pittsburgh	11	16
		(1905–06) Pittsburgh	18	23
Garnet Sixsmith	Ottawa, Ontario	(1904–05) Pittsburgh	2	1
		(1904–05) Canadian Soo	3	2
		(1905–06) Pittsburgh	14	7
Tommy Smith	Ottawa, Ontario	(1906–07) Pittsburgh	23	31
Charles "Baldy" Spittal	Ottawa, Ontario	(1904–05) Pittsburgh	23	2
		(1905–06) Canadian Soo	12	2
Joe Stephens	Seaforth, Ontario	(1904–05) Michigan Soo	24	14
Doug "Dad" Stewart	Whitby, Ontario	(1905–06) Canadian Soo	1	0
Fred Strike	Montreal, Quebec	(1904–05) Calumet	24	44
		(1905–06) Calumet	15	12
Bruce Stuart	Ottawa, Ontario	(1904–05) Portage Lake	22	33
		(1905–06) Portage Lake	20	15
		(1906–07) Portage Lake	23	20
William "Hod" Stuart	Ottawa, Ontario	(1904–05) Calumet	22	18
		(1905–06) Calumet	1	0
		(1905–06) Pittsburgh	20	11
		(1906–07) Pittsburgh	4	1
Boyd Sylvester	Lindsay, Ontario	(1904–05) Calumet	1	0
Fred Taylor	Tara, Ontario	(1905–06) Portage Lake	6	11
		(1906–07) Portage Lake	23	18

PLAYER	PLACE OF BIRTH	IHL TEAMS	GAMES	GOALS
Dunc Taylor	Toronto, Ontario	(1905–06) Pittsburgh	3	9
Bill "Lady" Taylor	Paris, Ontario	(1904–05) Canadian Soo (1905–06) Canadian Soo (1905–06) Michigan Soo (1906–07) Canadian Soo	24 10 4 24	35 13 5 46
Marty Walsh	Kingston, Ontario	(1906–07) Canadian Soo	7	4
Jack Ward	Rat Portage, Ontario (Kenora)	(1904–05) Canadian Soo (1905–06) Canadian Soo (1906–07) Michigan Soo	22 15 23	13 10 33
Ernie Westcott	Beaverton, Ontario	(1904–05) Portage Lake	3	0
Richard "Dick" Wilson	Kingston, Ontario	(1906–07) Canadian Soo (1906–07) Portage Lake	9 2	11 1
Jack Winchester	Belleville, Ontario	(1904–05) Pittsburgh (1905–06) Pittsburgh (1906–07) Pittsburgh	15 24 24	goalie goalie goalie
Fred "Bike" Young	Kingston, Ontario	(1904–05) Michigan Soo	2	0
Rowley Young	Toronto, Ontario	(1906–07) Pittsburgh	7	1

CHAPTER 8
After the International Hockey League

New Leagues Organize

By 1907, Canadian hockey had to face the growing reality of professionalism and several leagues were organized in which players were openly paid to pay hockey. Among the first leagues was the Ontario Professional Hockey League (OPHL). The OPHL was founded in November 1907 with four teams—the Berlin Dutchmen, Brantford Indians, Guelph Professionals, and the Toronto Professionals. Since the communities were connected by electric railway lines, the league became known as the "Trolley League." The Toronto team won the first league title and their top scorer was Newsy Lalonde. The Toronto team later joined the National Hockey Association (NHA). The OPHL operated for four seasons.

The Alberta Professional Hockey League (APHL) was also organized in 1907 with three teams—the Edmonton Pros, the Strathcona Shamrocks, and North Battleford. The league was basically inactive after one season when the teams from Strathcona and North Battleford folded but Edmonton played an exhibition schedule during the next two seasons and did challenge for the Stanley Cup in the 1908 and 1909 seasons, losing to the Montreal Wanderers and the Ottawa Senators of the Eastern Canada Amateur Hockey League (ECAHA). The league officially folded in 1910.

The third professional league was the Manitoba Professional Hockey League (MPHL). It was founded in 1906 and operated for three seasons. League teams included the Brandon Wheat Kings, Kenora Thistles, Portage la Prairie Cities, Winnipeg Strathconas, Winnipeg Maple Leafs, Winnipeg Shamrocks, and the Winnipeg Hockey Club. The Kenora Thistles defeated the Montreal Wanderers in January 1907 for the Stanley Cup, but were challenged and defeated a couple of months later by the same Wanderers team. In 1909, a challenge from the Winnipeg Shamrocks was accepted to play the Ottawa Senators of the ECAHA, but the series could not be arranged because it was late in the season.

Two semi-professional leagues formed during the 1907 expansion of professional hockey in Canada. The Temiskaming Hockey League operated for two seasons with teams in the Northern Ontario mining towns of Cobalt, Haileybury, and New Liskeard. The New Ontario Hockey League had teams from Schreiber, Fort William, and Port Arthur and operated for five seasons.

When the decision was made in the fall of 1907 to fold the IHL, the Pittsburgh–based Western Pennsylvania Hockey League (WPHL) was revived for the 1907–08 season with four teams—the Pittsburgh Lyceum, Pittsburgh Athletic Club, Pittsburgh Bankers, and Pittsburgh Pirates. The league was able to start the season early with the artificial ice surface in the Duquesne Gardens and teams signed several star players, but many of the players got better offers in December from teams in the new Canadian leagues so they left the league shortly after the season began. The same situation occurred in the 1908–09 season as star players defected to teams in Canada in mid-season for better salaries and the WPHL folded after the second season.

The Eastern Canada Amateur Hockey Association (ECAHA) was formed in 1906 with teams that had been members of the Canadian Amateur Hockey League and the Federal Amateur Hockey League. The league included teams from Ottawa, Quebec City, and Montreal (Wanderers, Victorias, AAA, and Shamrocks), and although the league had amateur in its title, the top players were being paid under the table. However, within a couple of years the league recognized the sham and allowed amateurs and professionals to play on the same team, as long as the owners made written declarations at the start of the season as to which players were amateurs and which were professionals. The Stanley Cup trustees also recognized the sham and in 1906 announced that professional teams could challenge for the Cup. In 1908, Sir Montagu Allan of Montreal donated a new hockey trophy for the best amateur team in Canada to replace the Stanley Cup and this trophy is known as the Allan Cup. Following the 1908–09 season, the ECAHA dissolved and reformed as the Canada Hockey Association (CHA), but the Montreal Wanderers were excluded from the new league so they decided to form a rival league, the National Hockey Association (NHA).

Sparked by the mining boom in Northern Ontario and the wealth of Renfrew businessman J. Ambrose O'Brien, the NHA was organized in the fall of 1909 with two teams from Montreal, and teams from Renfrew, Cobalt, and Haileybury. The league also decided to make some changes to the rules of hockey and introduced three 20 minute periods. During the organizational meeting, Jimmy Gardner, manager of the Montreal Wanderers, suggested a second team from Montreal comprised of French-speaking players. O'Brien enthusiastically supported the idea and provided financial backing to hire Jack Laviotte to assemble the team. The team would be known as the Montreal Canadiens. As soon as the league was formed, teams began to recruit players with salary offers higher

The Allan Cup was introduced in 1908 for the best amateur team in Canada to replace the Stanley Cup. (Government of Canada Library and Archives)

than had been seen before. O'Brien paid Lester Patrick $3,000, his brother Frank $2,000, and Fred Taylor $5,250 to play in Renfrew. Taylor's salary made him the second highest paid athlete in North America, second only to the Detroit Tigers outfielder Ty Cobb who was paid $6,500 for the season. The Renfrew team was officially called the Creamery Kings but they were known as the Millionaires. Within a month the new formed Canada Hockey Association (CHA) went out of business as league teams could not financially compete for the top players. The Ottawa Senators and Montreal Shamrocks were absorbed into the NHA. The Montreal Wanderers were the league's first champion. The cost of professional hockey had gotten out of hand and after the first season, the Montreal Shamrocks, Cobalt, and Haileybury folded. At the fall league meeting, a team salary cap was adopted and the rover position was eliminated. The Quebec Bulldogs joined the league for the second season and then two teams from Toronto (Blueshirts and Tecumsehs) were added for the third season.

In the fall of 1917, the NHA Board announced that due to a shortage of players they were suspending the league for the 1917–18 season. The Board was also troubled by the actions of Mr. Eddie Livingstone, owner of the Toronto Blueshirts. The owners of the Ottawa, Quebec, the two Montreal franchises (Canadiens and Wanderers), and the Toronto Arena Company met separately to explore setting up a new league, and they did not include Livingstone in the meetings. On November 26, 1917 the National Hockey League (NHL) was announced and the league would include five teams—Montreal Canadiens, Montreal Wanderers, Ottawa Senators, Quebec Bulldogs, and a new Toronto team. Quebec did not enter a team for the season and the arena where the Wanderers played burned down early in the season and they suspended operations, so the first NHL season finished with only three teams—the Montreal Canadiens, Ottawa Senators, and Toronto Arenas. The Arenas were the league's first champions and they defeated the Vancouver Millionaires, champions of the Pacific Coast Hockey Association (PCHA), in March 1918 in a five-game series for the Stanley Cup.

In 1911, Frank and Lester Patrick, bankrolled by millions made by their father in the lumber business in British Columbia, founded the Pacific Coast Hockey Association (PCHA) with three teams—New Westminister Royals, Vancouver Millionaires, and Victoria Aristocrats. The Patricks built new arenas in Vancouver and Victoria with artificial ice surfaces and were willing to pay the best players to head west. Jimmy Gardner, Hugh Lehman, Newsy Lalonde and Fred Taylor were among the top stars to be recruited for the league. The Patricks were innovators and introduced several changes in the game including blue lines and goal creases, forward passing, penalty shots, and playoffs. The league eliminated the rule that goaltenders must stay on their feet and introduced the use of sweater numbers to identify players. The Portland Rosebuds, Seattle Metropolitans, and Spokane Canaries would join the league in later years. At the end of the 1913–14 season, an agreement was made where the champions of the National Hockey Association and the PCHA would play for the Stanley Cup. Following the 1914–15 season, the PCHA champion Vancouver Millionaires defeated the NHA champion Ottawa Senators in a best-of-five series to become the first Stanley Cup champion from the PCHA. In 1916, the first American-based team, the Portland Rosebuds, played for the Stanley Cup but were defeated by the Montreal Canadiens and then in 1917, the Seattle Metropolitans became the first American-based team to win the Stanley Cup when they defeated the Montreal Canadiens.

In 1921, a second major professional league was organized in western Canada. In its first season, the Western Canada Hockey League (WCHL) included teams from Calgary, Edmonton, Regina, and Moose Jaw, and then in the second season, the WCHL played an interlocking schedule with the PCHA. When the Seattle Metropolitans folded after the 1923–24 season, the PCHA was left with two teams, the Vancouver Maroons and the Victoria Cougars. The PCHA disbanded and the Maroons and Cougars joined the WCHL. When Regina moved to Portland, the league was renamed the Western Hockey League (WHL) but only operated for one season (1925–26) before folding and reorganizing as a semi-professional league.

The league's playoff champion for the last season was the Victoria Cougars who would go on to face the Montreal Maroons for the Stanley Cup but were defeated in the series. When the WHL folded it also saw the end of the Stanley Cup as a competition between league champions, and the Cup would automatically be awarded to the NHL champion.

In the spring of 1926, a group of Detroit investors were granted a conditional expansion franchise to the NHL to begin play in the 1926–27 season if their arena was ready. The group purchased the players from the Victoria Cougars and although the arena was not ready, the NHL Board waived the condition and the franchise was awarded. The group kept the name Cougars and played their first season in Windsor, Ontario. The new Olympic Stadium was ready for the start of their second season. The team kept the Cougars name until 1930 when they became the Falcons for two seasons, and then in 1932 the team changed its name to the Red Wings.

The Chicago Black Hawks (now "Blackhawks") were also awarded NHL expansion franchise in the spring of 1926. The original investors purchased the players from the Portland Rosebuds and then within a month they sold the franchise to the Chicago coffee tycoon Frederic McLaughlin who named the team after a World War I military unit. The New York Rangers were also awarded a NHL expansion franchise that spring and began play in the 1926–27 season. The Boston Bruins were the first U.S. based NHL franchise when they began play in December 1924.

Destinations of IHL Players

When the IHL folded prior to the 1907–08 season, most of the league players returned to Canada to join a team in one of the new professional leagues. Members of the 1906–07 Portage Lake team signed contracts in several leagues.

Goldie Cochrane—Berlin Dutchmen (Ontario Professional Hockey League)

Grindy Forrester—Winnipeg Maple Leafs (Manitoba Professional Hockey League)

Barney Holden—Winnipeg Maple Leafs (Manitoba Professional Hockey League)

Fred Lake—Winnipeg Strathconas (Manitoba Professional Hockey League)

Darcy Regan—Winnipeg Maple Leafs (Manitoba Professional Hockey League)

Bruce Stuart—Montreal Wanderers (Eastern Canada Amateur Hockey Association)

Fred Taylor—Ottawa Senators (Eastern Canada Amateur Hockey Association)

Jack "Doc" Gibson was offered a contract to move to Johannesburg to introduce ice hockey in South Africa but he declined and moved to Calgary, Alberta where he entered into a real estate partnership with Charles S. Mills, a colleague from Southern Ontario who had also moved to Calgary. Gibson and Mills called their company the Alberta Locators and they acquired lands in Calgary and rural Alberta and expanded their firm to include general brokerage, insurance, and loans. Mills also became a Calgary automobile dealer. Gibson did not lose his passion for sports as he was a hockey referee and a member of the governing board of the Alberta Amateur Hockey Association and served a term as president. Gibson also played football for the Calgary Tigers and was a member when the team won the 1911 Western Canada Rugby Football Championship. Gibson joined the Canadian Army during World War I and served overseas with the 82nd Infantry Battalion. He was wounded in action at Courcelette, France. Following the war, he returned to Calgary and reopened his dental practice, continued his involvement in hockey and found many new interests. He was an avid curler and gardener. He was a member and past president of the Glencoe Club and the Calgary Horticultural Society. In 1950, at the age of 70, Gibson retired from dentistry as Calgary's most famous dentist. He died in 1954 and was survived by his wife Margaret, two sons and two daughters. For his contributions to hockey, Gibson was one of the original inductees into the United States Hockey Hall of Fame in 1973 and was inducted as a builder into the Hockey Hall of Fame in Toronto in 1976. One of the original trustees of the Stanley Cup, P.D. Ross, was inducted in the same class.

Gibson was not forgotten in Houghton and in 1938 members of the Northern Michigan-Wisconsin Hockey League purchased a trophy for the league's champion and named the Gibson Trophy or Cup in recognition of his outstanding contribution to hockey in its infancy in the Copper Country. The Gibson Cup was first awarded in 1939 to the Portage Lake Elks team and today the Gibson Cup is an annual competition trophy between two local senior amateur teams—the Portage Lake Pioneers and Calumet Wolverines.

Major Jack Gibson, 1914 (Jim and John Leech Collection)

Jack Gibson, 1954 (Jim and John Leech Collection)

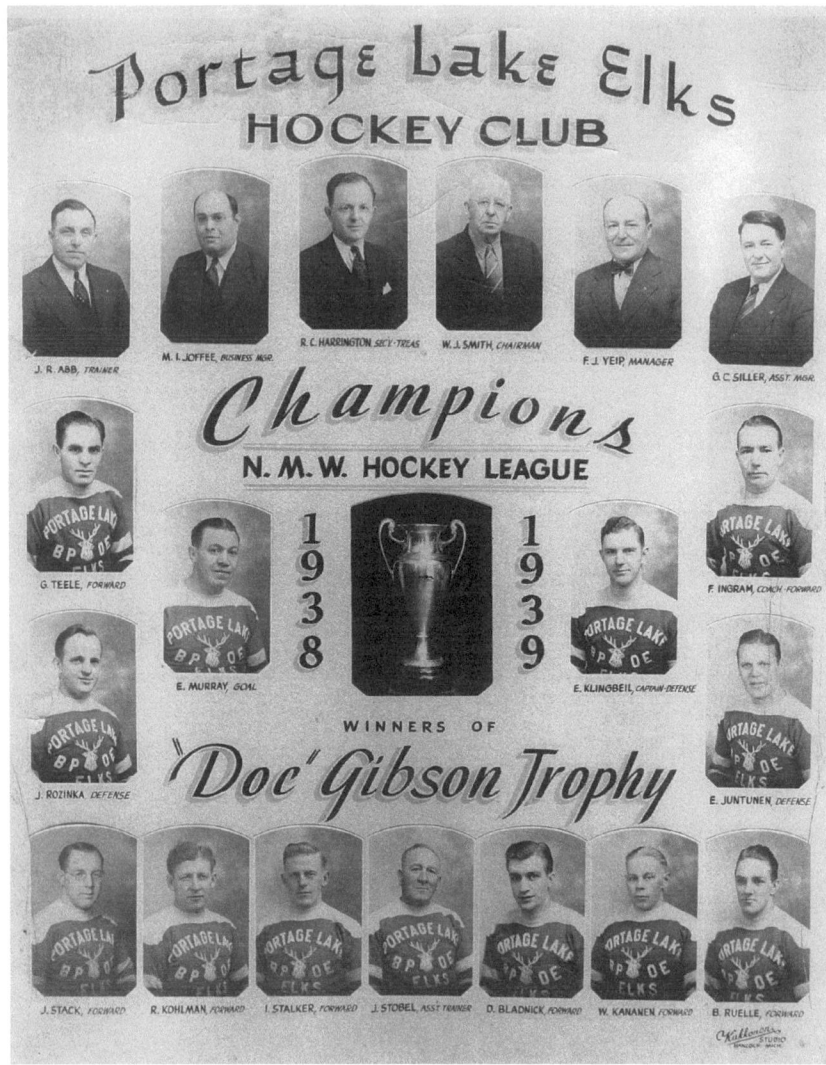

Portage Lake Elks Hockey Club—first team to win the Gibson Trophy (Michigan Technological University Archives and Copper Country Historical Collections)

Hockey in the Copper Country

The end of professional hockey did little to discourage interest in hockey in the Copper Country. Amateur hockey, particularly at the senior level, flourished and Portage Lake continued to have strong teams. In fact in 1913, Portage Lake defeated a team from Cleveland to win the U.S. Amateur Senior championship.

In 1907 an elaborate addition was built on the west end of the Amphidrome at a cost of $28,000 for an Armory and ballroom. A wooden exterior façade of castle towers was added and although the façade was like a movie set and had no useful purpose, it made for an impressive structure on the Houghton waterfront and in photographs. With the addition of the ballroom, the Amphidrome was the recreational and social center for numerous area events. Big bands from Chicago and Milwaukee as well as local bands played for dances. Great Lakes cruise ships docked next to the Amphidrome as passengers disembarked to visit downtown Houghton stores. A political rally for Teddy Roosevelt was held at the Amphidrome on October 9, 1912 and another rally was held later in the evening at the Palestra. Fire destroyed the Amphidrome on January 9, 1927, but through the efforts of Dee, the Amphidrome was rebuilt during the summer of 1927 and opened as the New Amphidrome in 1928. In 1942, the Michigan College of Mining and Technology bought the arena and changed its name to the James R. Dee Ice Stadium and in 1953 artificial ice was installed. When a new arena was opened on the Michigan Tech campus in 1972, the City of Houghton signed a lease agreement and eventually purchased the arena and today the City owns and operates Dee Stadium.

Construction of the new addition on the Amphidrome. (Michigan Technological University Archives and Copper Country Historical Collections)

In 1907, an addition was built on the west end of the Amphidrome for an Armory and ballroom. (Michigan Technological University Archives and Copper Country Historical Collections)

120 ● HOUGHTON: THE BIRTHPLACE OF PROFESSIONAL HOCKEY

A wooden exterior façade of castle towers were added for decorative purposes.
(Michigan Technological University Archives and Copper Country Historical Collections)

The Houghton County Fair was held in the fall at the Amphidrome
(Michigan Technological University Archives and Copper Country Historical Collections)

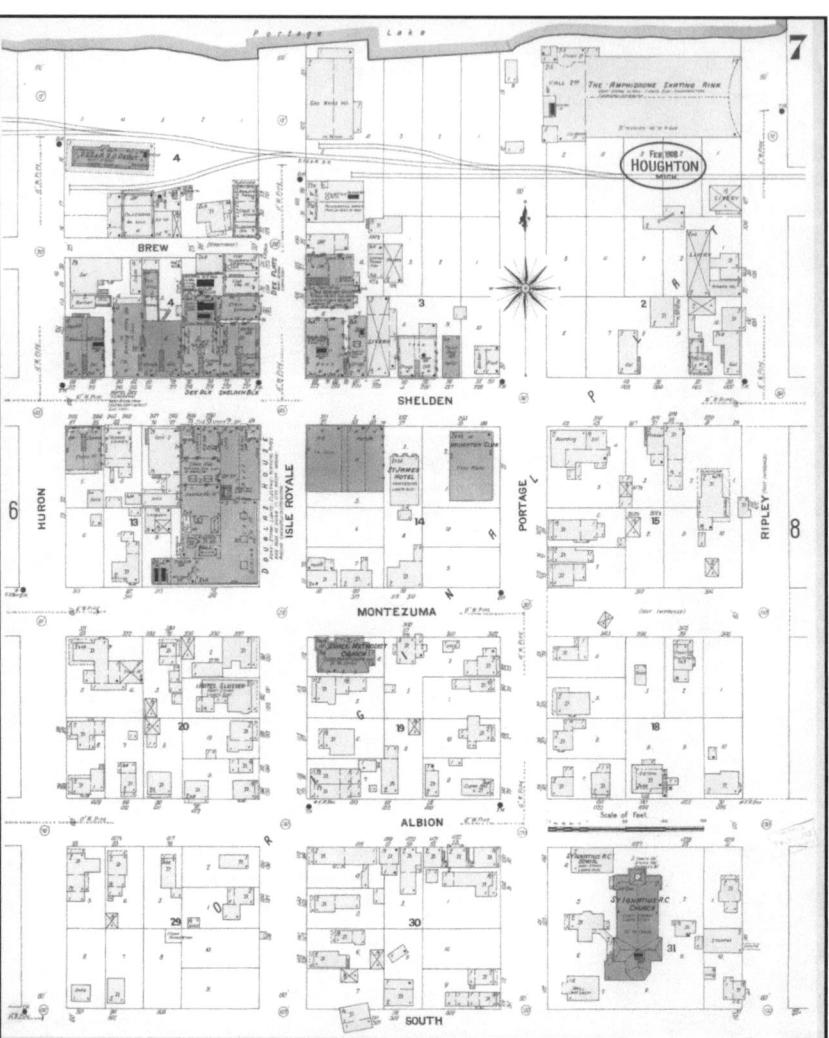

A Sanborn Fire Insurance Map (1908) showing the Amphidrome location on the Portage Lake waterfront. Note the location of the Houghton DSS&A railroad depot, the Douglass House, and the Shelden-Dee Building on Shelden at Isle Royale.

The Amphidrome was the recreational and social center of the community for numerous events. (City of Houghton Ralph Raffelli Collection)

122 ● HOUGHTON: THE BIRTHPLACE OF PROFESSIONAL HOCKEY

The Houghton waterfront with the Amphidrome in the 1920s. (Michigan Technological University Archives and Copper Country Historical Collections)

CHAPTER 8: AFTER THE INTERNATIONAL HOCKEY LEAGUE ● 123

The Amphidrome on the Houghton waterfront with the Quincy smelter in the foreground. A fire destroyed the Amphidrome on January 9, 1927. (Michigan Technological University Archives and Copper Country Historical Collections)

Dee organized a new company to rebuilt the arena and issued stock for the New Amphidrome (Michigan Technological University Archives and Copper Country Historical Collections)

New Amphidrome was built on the same waterfront location as the original Amphidrome. The building included a second floor ballroom but did not include the castle towers. (Michigan Technological University Archives and Copper Country Historical Collections)

In 1942, the Michigan College of Mining and Technology bought the arena and changed its name to the James R. Dee Ice Stadium.
(Michigan Technological University Archives and Copper Country Historical Collections)

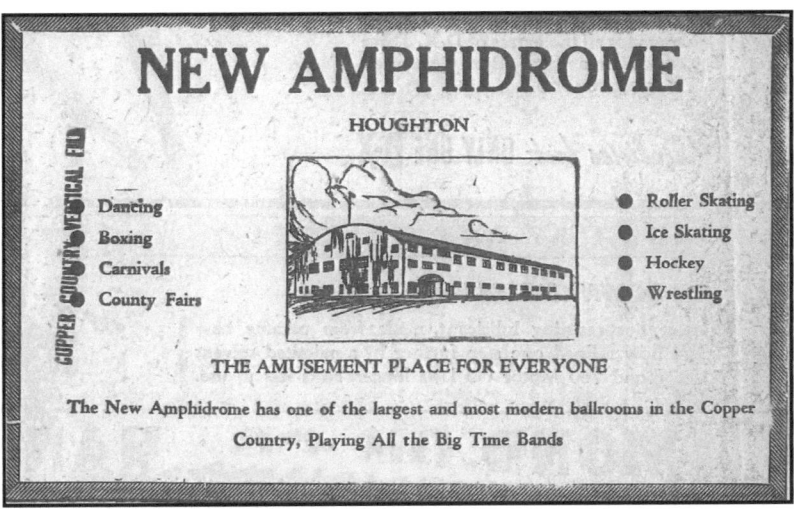

An advertisement for the New Amphidrome in Houghton Daily Mining Gazette, *1941.*

James R. Dee (Michigan Technological University Archives and Copper Country Historical Collections)

The Mohawk Glaciadom

In 1908 as hockey grew in the Copper Country, the Keweenaw Rink Company was formed to build a community building/arena in Mohawk for skating, hockey, dancing, bowling, and other community events. The building opened on December 28, 1908 and was given the name "Glaciadom" by Mrs. Alice Getchell. The Houghton County Traction Company had extended a streetcar line to Mohawk earlier in the year so frequent and dependable service was available to travel to other communities in the Copper Country. A Mohawk hockey team was organized in the first winter and Mohawk teams won Copper Country Senior Championships in 1910 and 1911. The Glaciadom closed in 1931 due to depressed economic conditions and six years later, during a heavy snow winter, the back portion of the roof collapsed. In the spring of 1938, the rest of the building was torn down and sold for scrap wood.

One of the top players on the Mohawk championship teams was Charles "Charlie" Uksila. Uksila (1887–1964) was born in Calumet and was one of the first American-born players to play in the Stanley Cup playoffs as a member of the 1915–16 Portland Rosebuds. He participated in hockey, figure skating, and speed skating while attending Calumet High School and later played left wing on the Mohawk team when they won the two championships. He would also put on skating performances and barrel-jumping demonstrations at the Glaciadom on Sunday afternoons during the hockey season. His mother and father were born in Finland and immigrated to the Copper Country and settled in the Calumet area in the early 1880s. His father was a laborer with the Osceola Mining Company, which would later become part of the Calumet and Hecla Mining Company. The family lived in Osceola and since there was a station on the Houghton County Traction Company streetcar line, it was easy for Uksila to travel to the Glaciadom. Charlie played professional hockey with the Portland Rosebuds of the Pacific Coast Hockey Association (PCHA) and during the era in which the champion of the PCHA would play the champion of the National Hockey Association (NHA) for the Stanley Cup. In March 1916, the Montreal Canadiens, NHA champions, beat Portland in five-game series in Montreal to win the Stanley

The Mohawk Glaciadom was built by the Keweenaw Rink Company in 1908 for skating, hockey, dancing, bowling, and community events.

(Michigan Technological University Archives and Copper Country Historical Collections)

Cup. This series marked the first time that an American-based team played for the Stanley Cup and the victory by the Canadiens was their first Stanley Cup championship. The Canadiens were an impressive team that included four players who were later inducted into the Hockey Hall of Fame—George Vezina, and three former IHL players, Newsy Lalonde, Jack Laviolette, and Didier Pitre. The Portland team included future Hockey Hall of Famers Ernie "Moose" Johnson and Tommy Dunderdale, the first Australia-born player to play for the Stanley Cup, and two American-born players—Tom Murray and Charlie Uksila.

As the Portland team traveled to Montreal, they stopped in Houghton for an exhibition game against a Michigan Upper Peninsula All-Star team of players from Portage Lake, Calumet, and Sault Ste. Marie, Michigan. The All Stars included future Hockey Hall of Famer Jack Adams. Adams played one season for Calumet, went on to play in the National Hockey League, and then had a long career as coach and general manager of the Detroit Red Wings. The game was played at the Amphidrome on March 17, 1916 with a final result of Portland 7 All Stars 6.

Calumet-born Charles "Charlie" Uksila in a Vancouver Millionaires uniform. He was one of the first American-born players to play in the Stanley Cup playoffs. (Houghton County Museum Archives)

Uksila played one season with the Vancouver Millionaires and among his teammates were former IHL players and future Hockey Hall of Famers Fred "Cyclone" Taylor and Hugh Lehmann. Taylor played two seasons with the Portage Lake team and Lehmann was goalie for one season with the Canadian Soo team. Charlie retired from hockey in 1919 and started a new career giving figure skating exhibitions in the United States and Australia, first with his sister Lenna, and then with his wife Dorothy ("Vida"). Charles and Vida performed at the Chicago World's Fair in 1933–34 and the 1939 New York World's Fair, and they toured with the world famous Norwegian figure skater Sonja Henie. Henie had won ten world skating championships and three Olympic gold medals when she retired to become a movie star and lead a professional skating touring company, the "Hollywood Ice Revue." She had numerous lucrative endorsement contracts to market skates, clothing, jewelry, and other merchandise branded with her name. These activities made Henie one of the wealthiest women in the world at that time. Charles also refereed NHL games during the 1930s and in 1940 he became a producer and choreographer for the newly formed "Ice Capades." Uksila died in California in 1964 and was inducted into the Michigan Upper Peninsula Sports Hall of Fame in 1974.

An advertisement in the Houghton Daily Mining Gazette *for a game between the Portland Rosebuds and the Michigan Upper Peninsula All Stars on Friday, March 17, 1916. The Portland team stopped in Houghton for a game while travelling to Montreal for a Stanley Cup championship series. At the time, some felt that Portland, by virtue of their league win over Vancouver, should have been awarded the Stanley Cup without the series (and declared World's Champions).*

HOCKEY!

WORLD'S CHAMPIONS
vs.
THE ALL STARS

TONIGHT
AT THE
AMPHIDROME

WE HAVE secured the World's Champions, we can get nothing better, and have got together a team that the fans are betting even money on that they will win.

Will you ever get a chance to see a world's championship again?

You can be sure of seeing the best game you ever seen, nothing like this game ever offered.

SEATS ON SALE AT

Nichols' Drug Store, Hancock
Alberts' Cigar Store, Houghton
First three rows . . . $1.00
Balance 75
General admission . . .50
Children 25

SPECIAL TRAINS

On the Copper Range from Calumet and Lake towns, also rates from L'Anse up.

Game Called at 8:30 sharp.

The Calumet Colosseum

In 1913, private investors financed the construction of a new arena in Red Jacket on a location close to the end of the Houghton County streetcar line on Sixth Street. The Calumet Colosseum opened on December 29, 1913 and the first hockey game was played between Calumet and Portage Lake senior teams on January 6, 1914 (Portage Lake defeated Calumet 4-2). The name was selected by the Directors of the Central Storage Company to recognize the size of the structure and it would be the fourth skating rink in the Copper Country with a classical name, the others being "Amphidrome", "Palestra", and "Glaciadom." In 1942, the Colosseum was sold to the State of Michigan following a fire at the local National Guard Armory. In need of a new building for the unit, the State purchased the Colosseum and changed its name to the Calumet Armory and for the next sixty years, the Calumet Hockey Association leased the ice surface during the winter season. Artificial ice was installed in 1968 and then in 2005, the National Guard moved to a new building and Calumet Township assumed ownership and restored the name of Colosseum. The Calumet Colosseum is the one of oldest hockey arenas in North America.

Following the opening of the Colosseum, Laurium's Palestra experienced a few years of disuse until a group from Marquette purchased the arena for $15,000, dismantled it, loaded it onto railcars, moved it by train, and then reassembled it to become Marquette's first indoor rink. The building was located at the corner of Third and Fair Streets on a site near Northern Michigan University's Berry Event Center. The arena was still called the Palestra and the first game in Marquette's Palestra was on December 22, 1921. The Palestra served the Marquette area for over fifty years before it was torn down after the Lakeview Arena opened in 1974.

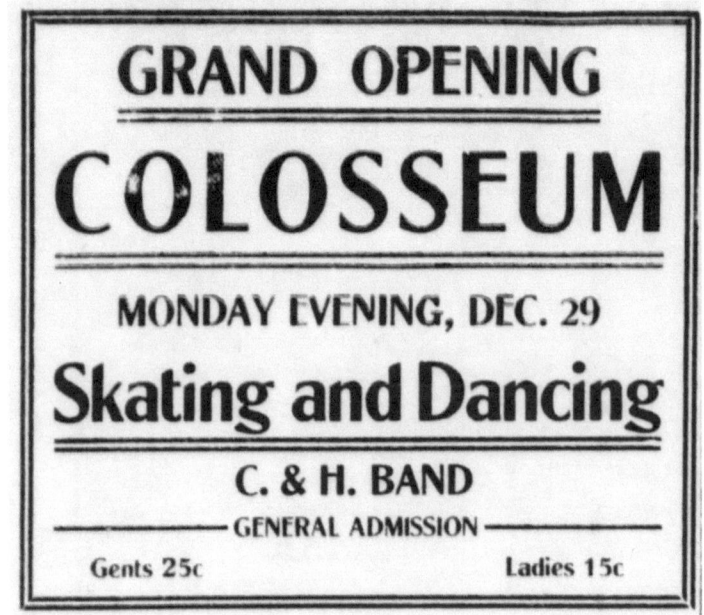

Advertisement in the Calumet News *for the Grand Opening of Colosseum on December 29, 1913.*

Following the opening of the Colosseum, the Palestra in Laurium experienced a few years of disuse until a group from Marquette purchased the building and moved it to Marquette. The first hockey game was played in the Marquette Palestra on December 22, 1921. (Houghton County Historical Society)

As hockey grew in the Copper Country a new arena was built in Red Jacket. The Calumet Colosseum was scheduled to open on December 29, 1913 but it was delayed by poor ice conditions. It opened for skating on January 1, 1914 and the first hockey game was played on January 6, 1914. It is one of the oldest hockey arenas in the United States. (Michigan Technological University Archives and Copper Country Historical Collections)

The MacNaughton Cup

Another important Copper Country hockey announcement was made on December 8, 1913 when James MacNaughton asked Charles Webb, president of the American Hockey Association, to purchase a trophy and present it to the Association's champion at the end of the season. The trophy has become known as the MacNaughton Cup. It was an interesting time in the Copper Country as the area was in the midst of the Copper Country Strike and it was a few weeks prior to the Italian Hall Christmas Eve disaster. The Calumet Colosseum was under construction and its grand opening was scheduled for December 29, 1913. Needless to say the announcement of the trophy did not receive extensive newspaper coverage.

At the time, MacNaughton was general manager of the Calumet and Helca Mining Company and was an avid supporter of amateur hockey. The first league to compete for the trophy was the American Amateur Hockey Association and its members included Calumet, Duluth, Portage Lake (Houghton), Sault Ste. Marie, Michigan, Sault Ste. Marie, Ontario, and teams from Cleveland and Boston. The first winner (1914) of the trophy was the Cleveland Athletic Club when they beat the team from Sault Ste. Marie, Michigan in league playoffs. The Cup was put into storage during World War I, but the winners of the Cup in these early years included teams from Sault Ste. Marie, Michigan, Sault Ste. Marie, Ontario, the St. Paul Athletic Club, and Eveleth, Minnesota. In the early 1930s, the Cup became a local trophy for competition in Michigan's Upper Peninsula and winners included teams from Hancock, Calumet, Ironwood, Painesdale, and Sault Ste. Marie, Michigan. There was no competition for the Cup during World War II and it went back into storage. In the early 1950s it was suggested that the Cup be offered to the newly formed Midwest Collegiate Hockey League, a precursor of the WCHA (Western Collegiate Hockey Association), for its league trophy. Endicott Lovell, president of the Calumet and Helca Mining Company at the time, was approached and he fully supported the idea and the league unanimously accepted the Cup. Lovell was also the son-in-law of James MacNaughton. The MacNaughton Cup has since been awarded annually to the season champion of the WCHA and Michigan Tech is the trophy's custodian.

James MacNaughton, General Manager of Calumet and Hecla Mining Company (Houghton County Museum Archives)

The MacNaughton Cup (Michigan Technological University Archives and Copper Country Historical Collections)

The International Hockey League Name Reappears

Although the International Hockey League only operated for the three seasons from 1904 to 1907, the name returned in 1929 when the Canadian Professional Hockey League (CPHL) split into two leagues. The larger teams formed the International Hockey League and the smaller teams kept the CPHL name and served as a farm system for the IHL. Among the original teams in the new IHL included Buffalo, Cleveland, Detroit, Hamilton, London, Niagara Falls, Toronto, and Windsor. However, after the 1935–36 season, several teams folded and the remaining teams merged with the CPHL to become the International American Hockey League. This new league would eventually become the American Hockey League (AHL) in 1940.

Another International Hockey League was founded in 1945 when a new IHL formed with four teams from Detroit and Windsor. The league expanded and contracted several times over the years and in the 1970s many of these teams were the top farm clubs of National Hockey League teams. In the late 1980s the IHL expanded into several major cities but many of the small-market teams left the league and joined lower-level leagues. The league expansion into some of the markets that had NHL franchises put a strain on the relationship between the IHL and NHL and many of the NHL teams shifted their farm team affiliations to the American Hockey League (AHL). With a loss of subsidized salaries and increasing travel and operating costs the latest International Hockey League folded after the 2000–01 season.

The Birthplace of Professional Hockey

Ice hockey has been part of the Copper Country culture since the game was introduced in the late 1890s. The Houghton area has been recognized as one the top hockey areas of the country and there were efforts in the 1970s to establish the United States Hockey Hall of Fame in Houghton County. It has been over a hundred years since the first professional hockey league was formed and how many would have guessed that a dentist from Canada would help to make a small town in northern Michigan the birthplace of professional hockey.

REFERENCES

Cameron, Steve (editor). *Hockey Hall of Fame Book of Players*. Firefly Books: Richmond Hill, Ontario, Second Edition, 2015.

Diamond, Dan (editor). *Total Hockey—The Official Encyclopedia of the National Hockey League*. Second Edition, Total Sports Publishing: Kingston, New York, 2000.

Dryden, Steve (editor). *Century of Hockey—A Season by Season Celebration*. The Hockey News/McClelland & Stewart Limited: Toronto, Ontario, 2000.

Duff, Bob. *The First Season: 1917–18 and the Birth of the NHL*. Biblioasis: Windsor, Ontario. 2017.

Farrell, Arthur. *Hockey: Canada's Royal Winter Game*, C.R. Corneil: Montreal, Quebec, 1899.

Fischler, Stan and Shirley. *Great Book of Hockey—More Than 100 Years of Fire on Ice*. Publications International Limited: Lincolnwood, Illinois, 1991.

Fitzsimmons, Ernie and James Milks, *The Players of the International Hockey League (1904 to 1907)*. Presented at Fall Meeting of the Society for International Hockey Research in Houghton, Michigan, September 1904.

Fitzsimmons, Ernie. *IHL Players—The Professional Pioneers*. In The Hockey Research Journal, Society for International Hockey Research, Volume VIII, 2004.

Fitzsimmons, Ernie. *Pittsburgh—The Cradle of Pro Hockey*. In The Hockey Research Journal, Society for International Hockey Research, Volume XIII, Fall 2009.

Fitzell, J.W. (Bill). *Doc Gibson—The Eye in the IHL*. In The Hockey Research Journal, Society for International Hockey Research, Volume VIII, 2004.

Fitzell, J.W. (Bill). *Hockey's Captains, Colonels & Kings*. Boston Mills Press: Erin, Ontario, 1897.

Fyffe, Iain. *On His Own Side of the Puck—The Early History of Hockey Rules*. Self-published, 2014.

Giden, Carl and Patrick Houda and Jean-Patrice Martel. *On the Origin of Hockey*. Hockey Origin Publishing: Stockholm, Sweden and Chambley, PQ, 2014.

Goodhand, Glen R. *The Many Faces of the International Hockey League*. In The Hockey Research Journal, Society for International Hockey Research, Volume XVI, 2012/13.

Haeussler, John S. *Hancock*. Arcadia Publishing: Charleston, SC, 2014.

Hardy, Stephen. *Polo at the Rinks: Shaping Markets for Ice Hockey in America, 1880–1900*. In Journal of Sports History, Volume 33, Number 2, Summer 2006.

Harper, Stephen J. *A Great Game—The Forgotten Leafs and the Rise of Professional Hockey*. Simon & Schuster Canada: Toronto, Ontario, 2013.

Hockey Hall of Fame (Toronto, Ontario)—Honoured Members, www.hhof.com.

Holden, Daniel T. *Cross Check!—Barney Holden and the Birth of Professional Hockey in North America*. Aventine Press: San Diego, CA, 2004.

Hubbard, Kevin and Stan Fischler. *Hockey America—The Ice Game's History, Growth and Bright Future in the U.S.* Masters Press: Indianapolis, IN, 1997.

Kitchen, Paul. *Rebels in Name Only—The Curious Story of an Ottawa Hockey Club, 1890–94*. In The Hockey Research Journal, Society for International Hockey Research, Volume XVI, 2012/13.

Lankton, Larry. *Cradle to Grave—Life, Work, and Death in Michigan's Copper Country*. Oxford University Press: New York, New York, 1991.

Mason, Daniel Scott. *The Origins and Development of the International Hockey league and its Effects on the Sport of Professional Ice Hockey in North America*. Master of Arts Thesis, University of British Columbia: Vancouver, BC, 1994.

Mason, Daniel S. *The International Hockey League and the Professionalization of Ice Hockey, 1904–1907*. In Journal of Sports History, Volume 25, Number 1, Spring 1998.

Mason, Daniel. *Hockey's First Professional Team: The Portage Lakes Hockey Club of Houghton, Michigan*. In Sports History Review, Volume 27, 1996.

Mason, Daniel S. and Gregory H. Duquette. *Newspaper Coverage of Early Professional Ice Hockey: The Discourses of Class and Control*. In Media History, Vol. 10, No. 3, 2004.

McKinley, Michael. *Hockey—A People's History*. McClelland & Stewart Limited: Toronto, Ontario, 2006.

McKinley, Michael. *Putting a Roof on Winter*. Greystone Books: Vancouver, BC, 2000.

Newspapers—*Calumet News, Copper Country Evening News, Daily Mining Gazette (Houghton), Pittsburgh Press, Calgary Herald*

Podnieks, Andrew. *Lord Stanley's Cup*. Fenn Publishing: Bolton, Ontario, 2004.

Ross, J. Andrew. *Joining the Clubs—The Business of the National Hockey League to 1945*. Syracuse University Press: Syracuse, New York, 2015.

Rubenstein, Bruce A. and Lawrence E. Ziewacz, *Michigan—A History of the Great Lake State*. Fifth Edition, John Wiley &Sons: Malden, MA, 2014.

Shubert, Howard. *Architecture on Ice—A History of the Hockey Arena*. McGill-Queen's University Press: Montreal/Kingston, 2016.

Slater, Kevin. *Trolley League—The Complete History of the Ontario Professional Hockey League*. Self-published, 2010.

Society for International Hockey Research (SIHR) database of teams and players—www.sihrhockey.org.

Sproule, William J. *Copper Country Streetcars*. Arcadia Publishing: Charleston, SC, 2013.

Sproule, William J. *The MacNaughton Cup—One of Hockey's Oldest Active Trophies*. In The Hockey Research Journal, Society for International Hockey Research, Volume VIII, 2004.

Sproule, William J. *The Allan Cup—Hockey's Second Oldest Trophy*. In The Hockey Research Journal, Society for International Hockey Research, Volume XIV, Fall 2010.

Taylor, Richard E. *Houghton County 1870–1920*. Arcadia Publishing: Charleston, SC, 2006.

Thurner, Arthur. *Calumet Copper and People—History of a Michigan Mining Community 1864–1970*. Self-published, 1974.

Thurner, Arthur W. *Strangers and Sojourners—A History of Michigan's Keweenaw Peninsula*. Wayne State University: Detroit, Michigan, 1994.

U.S. Hockey Hall of Fame (Eveleth, Minnesota)—Inductees, www.ushockeyhalloffame.com.

Vaughan, Garth. *The Puck Starts Here*. Goose Lake: Fredericton, NB, 1996.

Wernig, Darin. *Gateway City Puckchasers—The History of Hockey in St. Louis*. Wernig Media: St. Louis, Missouri, 2014.

Whitehead, Eric. *Cyclone Taylor—A Hockey Legend*. Doubleday: Toronto, Ontario, 1977.

Wong, John Chi-Kit. *Lords of the Rinks—the Emergence of the National Hockey League 1875–1936*. University of Toronto Press: Toronto, Ontario, 2005.

Zweig, Eric. *Bad Joe—The Life and Times of a Hockey Legend*. In The Hockey Research Journal, Society for International Hockey Research, Volume XIII, Fall 2009.

Zweig, Eric. *Fever Season*. Dundurn Press: Toronto, Ontario, 2009.

Zweig, Eric. *Setting Cyclone's Story Straight*. In The Hockey Research Journal, Society for International Hockey Research, Volume XI, Fall 2007.

Zweig, Eric. *Star Power—The Legend and Lore of Cyclone Taylor*. Lormier Publishing: Toronto, Ontario, 2007.

www.ingramcontent.com/pod-product-compliance
Lightning Source LLC
Chambersburg PA
CBHW041644070526
44585CB00004B/124